P9-DMQ-734

TALES FROM THE
BOSTON BRUINS
LOCKER ROOM

TALES FROM THE
BOSTON BRUINS
LOCKER ROOM

A COLLECTION OF THE GREATEST
BRUINS STORIES EVER TOLD

KERRY KEENE

SPORTS
PUBLISHING

Sports Publishing books may be purchased in bulk at special discounts for sales promotion, corporate gifts, fund-raising, or educational purposes. Special editions can also be created to specifications. For details, contact the Special Sales Department, Sports Publishing, 307 West 36th Street, 11th Floor, New York, NY 10018 or info@skyhorsepublishing.com.

Sports Publishing® is a registered trademark of Skyhorse Publishing, Inc.®, a Delaware corporation.

www.skyhorsepublishing.com

10 9 8 7 6 5 4 3 2 1

Library of Congress Cataloging-in-Publication Data is available on file.

ISBN: 978-1-61321-058-1

Printed in the United States of America

ACKNOWLEDGMENTS

In keeping with a hockey theme, assists must be credited to Steve Babineau, Peter Curry, Fred Cusick, David Flebotte, Dick Johnson of the Sports Museum of New England, Rene Rancourt, Dick Sarkisian of the Sports Tradition in West Bridgewater, Massachusetts, and Bob Sweeney and Mal Viola of the Boston Bruins Alumni Association.

Nominees for my Most Valuable Player go to David Hickey, Harvey McKenney, and Kevin Vautour.

CONTENTS

Preface:
The Long Awaited Reunion with Lord Stanley's Cup

Often, there is a more compelling story of the journey than of the arrival.

On June 15, 2011, the Boston Bruins, rising to the heights of their capabilities and perhaps a bit beyond, shifted many painful memories and bitter disappointments to a less prominent place in the minds of a legion of followers. But at that precise moment, it was nearly impossible not to look back to a simpler time when the thought of such an expedition seemed far less daunting.

The scene fades to New York's Madison Square Garden, May 11, 1972. The Bruins skate around the ice with the Stanley Cup—the second time they have captured the coveted trophy in three years. With figures such as Bobby Orr and Phil Esposito solidly in their prime and an outstanding supporting cast around them, it was reasonable to assume that this scene would be repeated a few more times as the decade unfolded.

Entering the Stanley Cup Finals in June, 2011, no lifelong Bruins' fan under the age of forty-two could possibly possess a personal, firsthand memory of the team winning the elusive prize, or the subsequent victory parade through the streets of Boston.

But even as that parade was rolling in the spring of '72 celebrating the beloved Bruins, the landscape of professional hockey was in the process of being altered forever. Not only was the National Hockey League set to add two new teams—the New York Islanders and the Atlanta Flames—the World Hockey Association was set to begin its inaugural season in the fall, with twelve new teams poised to compete directly with the NHL for both players and fans.

As the Bruins were set to open the 1972-'73 season to defend their Stanley Cup championship, they would be doing so without key players such as goaltender Gerry Cheevers, who signed with Cleveland of the WHA; Derek Sanderson, who signed a lavish deal with the new circuit's Philadelphia team; Ted Green and Johnny McKenzie jumped to the league's nearby New England Whalers; and Eddie Westfall, who was lost to the Islanders in the expansion draft. The team that the entire Boston area had fallen head over heels for the previous few seasons had lost several of its key components and would never again be able to replicate the success of 1972. The Bruins franchise would continue to retain its extraordinarily loyal fan base, but for the next few decades, they would live in the formidable shadow of those Stanley Cup winners from the early 1970s. They possessed a unique blend of sheer talent and a cast of true characters that had proven to be virtually impossible to duplicate.

Reprising even one of those unforgettable Stanley Cup victories over these many years has proven to be as elusive as the fabled unicorn, the pot of gold at the end of the rainbow, or Captain Ahab's white whale.

Eleven months after hoisting the Cup in '72 at Madison Square Garden, the Bruins were unceremoniously eliminated from the playoffs in the first round in six games by those same Rangers. The recently departed Bruins stars had taken a bit of the team's magic with them.

The next season the Bruins bounced back and celebrated the franchise's 50th season with a better performance in '73-'74 and managed to get back to the Stanley Cup Finals. They were beaten, however, by the upstart Philadelphia Flyers in six games. Led by center Bobby Clarke and goaltender Bernie Parent, the "Broad Street Bullies" also won the following season's Stanley Cup. With that Cup victory in 1975, the Flyers had won as many in their eight-season existence as Boston had won in the previous thirty-three years.

The Bruins were clearly one of the elite teams in the NHL in the decade of the 1970s, finishing either first or second in their division every season. But by 1977, the nucleus of the team was dramatically different from the Stanley Cup winning teams from earlier in the decade. Though Cheevers had returned to the team in early '76 and Johnny Bucyk and Wayne Cashman remained, gone were Orr, Esposito, Ken Hodge, Fred Stanfield, Eddie Johnston, and Don Awrey. In their places were Brad Park, Jean Ratelle, Peter McNab, Rick Middleton, and Mike Milbury, with the popular and outspoken Don Cherry behind the bench.

In May of '77 Boston advanced to the Stanley Cup Finals, but had the unenviable task of facing a Montreal team that was not only the defending Cup champion but who had won sixty games in the regular season while losing only eight. The series was over quickly as the juggernaut Canadiens swept the Bruins in four straight games.

The two teams had a return engagement in the finals the following spring, 1978. The Canadiens were only slightly less dominant that season, winning 59 and losing 10. After losing the first two games in Montreal, the Bruins managed to tie the Series with wins in Games 3 and 4 back at the Boston Garden. But Montreal came back with wins in Games 5 and 6 to capture the third of what would be four straight Cups for the Canadiens.

But it was Boston's exit from the playoffs in the spring of 1979 that Boston Red Sox fans might relate to as the Bruins "Bucky Dent" or "Bill Buckner moment."

Ahead by one goal in Game 7 with two-and-a-half minutes to go in the Conference Finals against their old nemesis, Montreal, fate would intervene in a cruel way.

At that moment, a penalty was called on Boston for "too many men on the ice." The call elicits a collective groan to this day from every Bruins fan who observed it. Despite a gallant effort, the Bruins could not hang on to kill off the penalty. With less than a minute and a half remaining in regulation time, the Canadiens' star right-winger, Guy Lafleur, put a slapshot past Bruins goaltender Gilles Gilbert. Nearly ten minutes into overtime, Canadiens' left-winger Yvan Lambert's goal helped Montreal send the Bruins home empty-handed for the third straight year. Compounding the anguish for Bruins' fans was the realization that had Boston hung on to win Game 7 to advance to the Finals, they would have met a New York Rangers team that many felt was inferior to the

Bruins. Boston had finished the regular season with nine more points than New York, and had beaten the Rangers in three of their five meetings. Montreal went on to dispatch New York in five games to win their fourth straight Stanley Cup. Bruins' fans were left to ponder "what if . . . "

The loss further rekindled the horrific memory of being eliminated by Montreal in the playoffs back in 1971. The defending Stanley Cup-winning Bruins had put together what was likely their greatest season both collectively and individually before or since. They took their 57 wins and 121 points into the opening round versus the Canadiens (46 wins, 97 points). In goal for Montreal was rookie Ken Dryden, who had only appeared in six games in the regular season. Dryden's performance in goal was stellar, and Boston went home stunned after a Game 7 loss.

As the decade of the '80s was getting underway, the team was adding young players who could potentially form a great nucleus for the future. The month after their disheartening defeat at the hands of Montreal in May of '79, Boston drafted defenseman Ray Bourque in the first round of the amateur draft. They would add center Barry Pederson in the '80 draft, the ill-fated Normand Leveille in '81, and defenseman Gord Kluzak in '82. These and other youngsters such as Steve Kasper and Mike Krushelynski were set to blend with veterans Middleton, Peter McNabb, Brad Park, and Terry O'Reilly.

On April 25, 1982, the Bruins failed to advance beyond the second round of the playoffs for the third consecutive year with a Game 7, 2-1 loss to Quebec. It ultimately became the final game played by left-winger Don Marcotte, who wrapped up his 15-season NHL career spent entirely in a Bruins uniform. Now ten years since Boston last skated with the Cup, only veteran Wayne Cashman remained from that magical team. One year later, Cashman would play his last game, and the original "Big, Bad Bruins" took their place in team history.

In Cashman's last playoff series in May of 1983, Boston made it all the way to Game 6 of the Wales Conference Finals, defeated by the powerful three-time defending Stanley Cup champion New York Islanders. Again, it was another big "what if" for Bruins fans. Had Boston been able to get by the Islanders and advance to the Finals, many felt they had a decent chance at beating Edmonton. Though the Oilers featured a young Wayne Gretzky and an equally young Mark Messier, the team was inexperienced, making its first appearance in the Finals. They had won three less regular season games than the Bruins had while playing in the weaker Campbell Conference. In their three regular season meetings that year, Boston had won two and tied one. The Islanders went on to a four-game sweep of Edmonton, earning their fourth consecutive title.

Throughout the mid-1980s it was firmly established for a generation of Bruins fans that the Montreal Canadiens were to the Bruins what the New York Yankees had been to the Boston Red Sox. All roads to the Stanley Cup seemed to go through Montreal, and the Bruins were finding every dead end. For four straight years, from 1984 through 1987, the Bruins were eliminated in the first round of the playoffs by "Les Habs." Boston's combined record over those four series against Montreal was 2-12. In the twenty seasons from the spring of 1968 through the spring of '87, the Bruins were bounced by Montreal ten times.

The tide finally turned a year later in the second round of the 1988 playoffs. The Bruins got a rather large monkey off their back by beating Montreal in a playoff series for the first time in forty-five years. Boston had finished in second place in the Adams Division, 9 points behind the Canadiens, but the playoffs told a different story. Led by Bourque, Cam Neely, Ken Linseman, and goalie Reggie Lemelin, the Bruins knocked out their arch-rivals in five games. They lost the opening game in Montreal, 5-2, but won the next four by a combined score of 13-5. It was tremendously liberating for the Bruins and their fans to finally prevail against their hated rivals.

Boston kept rolling, beating the New Jersey Devils in seven games in the Conference Finals. They earned the right to face Edmonton in the Cup Finals in May of '88, their first Finals appearance in ten years. The Oilers, led by Gretzky, Messier, and goaltender Grant Fuhr, had won the Cup three of the previous four years. They proved to be too strong, beating the Bruins in each of the first three games. The fourth game, at the Boston Garden, was tied 3-3 when a transformer blew, causing a blackout. Power was unable to be restored, and the game was suspended. Two days later back in Edmonton, the Oilers skated away with their fourth Cup in five seasons. It would be the final game Gretzky would play for Edmonton, as he was traded to the Los Angeles Kings less than three months later.

As a result of the mechanical problems that occurred in the ancient Boston Garden that May, talk of replacing it became more serious. It would take eight more years before the old barn gave way to the New Fleet Center (now known as TD Garden).

A year after their loss in the '88 Finals to Gretzky and company, the Bruins revisited the painful experience of being eliminated by the Canadiens once again. This time it came in the second round in five games.

Led by rookie coach Mike Milbury the following season, the 1989-'90 edition of the Bruins was their most powerful in years. They topped the NHL in victories and points, led by Neely's 55 goals, Norris Trophy-winning defense from Bourque, and a great goaltending tandem of Lemelin and Andy Moog. They earned a re-match of the Finals of two years prior with a chance for revenge against Edmonton, now led by Messier, Jari Kurri, and former (and future) Bruins' goaltender Bill Ranford.

The results were not much better this time around, however, as it took only five games for the Oilers to dispose of the Bruins. Boston managed to win Game 3 by a slim 2-1 margin, but were ousted two games later in what was to be the last Stanley Cup Final ever held at the old Boston Garden.

Though the Bruins would advance to the Conference Finals the next two seasons, and their future appeared bright, they were set to embark on what would be their longest drought of Stanley Cup Finals appearances in the history of the franchise. As the years marched onward, the Bruins experienced many noteworthy occurrences, events, performances, player transactions, and coaching changes, but none of them seemed to put the team in the best-of-seven series that could earn them the Cup. The following two decades were marked more by a variety of happenings that generally had little to do with capturing the sport's ultimate prize. The 1994-'95 season was cut down to 48 games due to a labor dispute. September of '95 saw the closing of the old Garden and the opening of the new Fleet Center. January of '96 provided a thrill when the new arena hosted the annual All-Star Game, with Ray Bourque scoring the winning goal with a half-minute remaining. 1997 saw something the Bruins hadn't done in thirty years. They missed the playoffs and finished with the worst record in the NHL. The positive side to that was drafting popular young potential superstar Joe Thornton first overall in June, 1997. They also had the eighth pick in that draft's first round, which they used to select Russian left-winger Sergei Samsonov.

Boston made it back to the playoffs the following spring, but were dismissed by the Washington Capitals in the opening round. They made it to the second round in 1999, but were sent home by Buffalo in six games.

The Bruins suffered a terrible season in '99-2000, and in early March, when a playoff spot was out of reach, they made a painful decision. They traded the thirty-nine-year-old Bourque to Colorado to provide him with a chance to finally win a Stanley Cup. His new team fell one game shy of making the Finals that spring, but one year later, in a bittersweet scene for Bruins fans, Bourque finally won his Cup in an Avalanche uniform.

As the 21st century arrived, the Bruins were entering a decade that would almost rival the futility of the dark days from the 1959-'60 season through 1966-'67. From the spring of 2000 through 2009, they missed making the playoffs four times (excluding the 2004-'05 season, which was cancelled by another labor dispute). On the five occasions during that span that they did qualify for the playoffs, they got past the first round only once.

Finally, in the spring of 2010, Boston looked like they were on the verge of making a serious run at the Cup. They beat Buffalo four games to two in the opening round of the playoffs. They then took a commanding three-games-to-none lead over Philadelphia in the second round when fate intervened once again. Against overwhelming odds, the Flyers were able to chip away, one game at a time, and found themselves tied three games apiece, forcing a Game 7.

Boston jumped out to an early 3-0 lead in that final match, but by the third period, the Flyers had crept back to tie the score. Late in the game, when overtime appeared a distinct possibility, a ghost from 1979 came to haunt the new Garden. The Bruins were again called for "too many men on the ice" and were unable to kill the penalty as Simon Gagne scored to put the Flyers ahead to stay, 4-3. The Bruins and their fans were stunned. It was only the third time in NHL history a team had blown a three-games–to-none lead.

It was a horrible way to celebrate the 40th anniversary of Bobby Orr's historic Stanley Cup-winning goal.

Five months later, the 2010-'11 Bruins had to find a way to put their colossal collapse behind them to begin a new quest in a new season.

This particular edition began to add its important components years before, when it signed a journeyman minor league goaltender named Tim Thomas. He would make his NHL debut with Boston in 2002 at nearly twenty-nine years old, and would spend significant time with the Bruins minor league team in Providence over the next few seasons. His rise to being one of the top goalies in the league is a remarkable story of perseverance.

General manager Mike O'Connell added more key players in the amateur drafts, picking center Patrice Bergeron in

2003 and center David Krejci in '04. After O'Connell's dismissal, interim G.M. Jeff Gorton added both Milan Lucic and Brad Marchand through the 2006 draft. Two weeks before the Bruins officially hired Peter Chiarelli as their new G.M., the team made one of its most significant acquisitions by signing free agent all-star defenseman Zdeno Chara.

The team had hired coach Dave Lewis before the '06-'07 season, but Chiarelli cut his losses with Lewis after just one year and brought in former Devils and Canadiens coach Claude Julien. The general manager also executed several key trades over the next few years, bringing in right wingers Michael Ryder and Mark Recchi, center Nathan Horton, and defensemen Andrew Ference, Johnny Boychuk, and Dennis Seidenberg. Chiarelli had also traded young center Phil Kessel in 2009 for a draft pick that turned out to be center Tyler Seguin.

Boston's 46 regular season victories helped them finish tied for fourth in their conference with 103 points. But simply making the playoffs wasn't going to make up for the previous season's shocking end. The task began with an opening round against the always challenging Canadiens. The Bruins quickly found themselves down 0-2 in the series, but came back to win in seven games, including three victories in overtime.

They then exacted revenge against the Philadelphia team that embarrassed them the spring before by sweeping them in four straight games. It was on to Tampa Bay to face the Lightning in the Conference Finals. It was an incredibly hard-fought series with two teams that appeared fairly evenly matched. In the end, the Bruins prevailed in a spectacular Game 7 with a late goal for a 1-0 win and at last, a return trip to the Stanley

Cup Finals, where they'd face the President's Cup-winning Vancouver Canucks.

Slightly favored entering the series, Vancouver and their top goaltender, Roberto Luongo, jumped out to a two games-to-none lead, with both games won by a one-goal margin. An incident that occurred in Game 2 served as a spark and a rallying cry for Boston, however. A brutal hit by Canuck defenseman Aaron Rome on forward Nathan Horton saw Horton taken off on a stretcher, lost for the remainder of the series with a severe concussion. Boston would come back in the next two games at home and send a clear message by beating Vancouver 8-1 and 4-0.

Back in British Columbia for Game 5, both goaltenders were tremendous, but the Canucks squeaked by with a 1-0 win. The Bruins, facing elimination as the series shifted back to Boston, regained the upper hand with a 5-3 win in Game 6. They were now poised to return to Vancouver for what would be their first Game 7 in a Stanley Cup Final in their long and storied history.

For the entire series, the Bruins were able to basically neutralize Vancouver's top offensive threats, Ryan Kesler and the Sedin twins, Henrik and Daniel. Also at times, they made Luongo look very beatable in net. These trends were in full force in Game 7 as Boston dominated virtually every aspect of play. Bergeron and Marchand each scored twice, and Marchand's empty net goal with 2:44 left sealed the victory, a 4-0 shutout.

On June 15, 2011, at 7:45 PM Pacific Standard Time, Boston's beloved hockey team had ended a drought that had lasted 14,279 days by bringing home Hockey's Holy Grail. For the long-suffering Garden faithful, the words "2011 Stanley Cup Champion Boston Bruins" had a marvelous, glorious ring to them.

—Kerry Keene
June 15, 2011

INTRODUCTION

As the research for this particular body of work began, I thought to comb my own personal archives for various material that might be helpful in recounting interesting and significant moments, incidents, memories, highlights, and milestones from the tremendous history of the Boston Bruins hockey club. Having been a follower of the team for 35 years, I was certain that I had accumulated numerous keepsakes that might provide a significant glimpse into the past of a beloved team that had meant so much to so many.

In digging through the assorted items, I did indeed come across a grand total of 13 different Boston Bruins yearbooks; various souvenir game night programs; hardcover autobiographical works written by Phil Esposito, Bobby Orr, Johnny Bucyk, Derek Sanderson, and Ted Green; bubble gum hockey cards of Orr and teammates; autographed glossy photos of a few Bruins; a Boston Bruins tie pin—circa 1971—"Goal: Bruins," a 33 1/3 rpm record album documenting the 1969-70 season, and even two original seats from the Boston Garden.

It occurred to me that the Boston Bruins hockey team had long ago ingrained itself as almost a part of the family, as familiar, as significant, and as relevant as many actual members of the family. In short, no claims are being made by the author of neutrality, non-bias, or of being a disinterested party whose goal is to simply report the facts.

I was initially exposed to Bruins hockey in the fall of 1967 on Boston's TV channel 38 and became almost instantly hooked on the team and the game. The local station had brought the team into thousands upon thousands of New England homes, and in time the boys in black and gold became more popular among sports fans than their Red Sox and Celtics brethren.

I observed the games almost exclusively for three full seasons through channel 38, save for the occasional nationally televised game on a Sunday afternoon. Finally, in the fall of 1970, six months after that glorious Stanley Cup victory, my parents decided it was time to view our heroes in person in the confines of the classic old Boston Garden. The night, November 26, made such an impression that it still stands out in my memory. I was proud to be one of the announced 14,994 in attendance, and it was almost surreal when the Bruins skated out onto the ice for warmups. One by one, it was so easy to pick them out as they came to life less than 75 feet away.

It didn't take long after the opening faceoff for the old Garden to erupt. A minute and a half into the game, none other than Bobby Orr himself put the puck past the Blackhawks goaltender. Goosebumps were raised further when PA announcer Frank Fallon bellowed out "Boston goal by number four, Bobby Orr!"

There were other memorable moments to bring the crowd to its feet. Boston goals were also scored by Johnny McKenzie and Johnny Bucyk, and the colorful Derek Sanderson got into a fight with one of the true arch-villains of the era, Chicago defenseman Keith Magnuson. A 3-2 Bruins victory ensured a happy ending and a memory to last a lifetime. I had witnessed what I believed to be a fairly recent phenomenon

TALES FROM THE
BOSTON BRUINS
LOCKER ROOM

CHARLES F. ADAMS

Charles Adams should never be forgotten or overlooked as the true father of the Boston Bruins franchise. A native New Englander born in Newport, Vermont, near the Canadian border on October 17, 1876, he migrated to Boston and became a successful businessman. An avid sportsman, he attended the Stanley Cup Finals in Montreal in the spring of 1924 and was determined to bring the National Hockey League to Boston.

Adams was able to purchase what was essentially an expansion franchise for Boston on October 12, 1924 for $15,000 and set about putting together the first American-based team in league history. He was impressed by the hockey credentials of Art Ross, who had served as a referee at the 1924 finals and who had starred in several professional leagues in the early part of the century. Adams immediately hired the 38-year-old Ross to be the first coach and general manager of his newly formed Boston ice hockey team.

Adams wanted the team to have a nickname that reflected the qualities of strength, ferocity, and cunning and also wanted to utilize a color scheme of brown and gold that were the colors used in his Boston-area Brookside grocery stores. Coach Ross's secretary submitted the name "Bruins," and the team that has been such a big part of NHL history was born.

For the next half-century, the Adams family was involved in the running of the Bruins franchise. Though Adams was also renowned in Boston sporting circles as the owner of the Suffolk Downs Race Track and as a co-owner of the Braves baseball team, it is the city's legendary ice hockey team that always remain his lasting legacy.

Weston Adams Sr.

The son of Charles Adams, Weston attended Harvard University and played goalie for the Crimson hockey team. He also served in the 1930s as the traveling secretary for his father's Boston Braves baseball team. Weston assumed the presidency of the Bruins in the late 1930s, and would be succeeded by his son Weston Jr. in 1969.

When the Bruins had missed the playoffs for a couple of years in the early 1960s, Weston Sr. decided to go on scouting missions all across Canada. It was on one of these trips while in Ganonoque, Ontario, initially to scout two players named Eaton and Higgins, that he first saw a youngster named Bobby Orr. Eaton and Higgins were quickly forgotten, and the pursuit of the 14-year-old phenom Orr began in earnest.

Johnny Aiken

In the earlier decades of the NHL, teams often did not travel with a backup goalie in order to keep expenses down. On March 13, 1958, with Montreal visiting the Boston Garden, Canadiens goalie Jacques Plante was injured early in the second period and was unable to continue. Montreal borrowed Bruins practice goalie Johnny Aiken to finish the game, which was not an altogether unheard-of practice at the time.

Aiken allowed six goals to be scored by the team he usually practiced against as the Bruins went on to win 7-3. This may not have helped his chances of becoming a regular

2

goalie. He had made the only appearance he would ever make in an NHL game that night.

GARNET "ACE" BAILEY

The memory of Ace Bailey was brought back to Bruins fans in the most tragic manner possible when it was learned that he was aboard United Airlines Flight #175 that crashed into the World Trade Center in New York City on September 11, 2001. Ace had been living in Lynnfield, Massachussetts at the time, and was working as a scout for the Los Angeles Kings. Bruins assistant coach Wayne Cashman recalled having a lengthy telephone conversation with him the day before his death.

The forward was a very well liked and funloving character and member of the 1970 and '72 Stanley Cup Bruins teams. Coach Tom Johnson had said of him back then, "Ace likes his fun, but once the game starts, he's all business." Playing center on the fourth line in the '72 Finals against the Rangers he scored the winning goal in Game One. One of his teammates had said before the Finals began that if Bailey played regularly he'd be a 30-goal scorer.

In training camp at London, Ontario, in the fall of 1968, Gerry Cheevers recalled sitting with fellow goalie Eddie Johnston watching Ace flying around the ice hitting players and asked, "Who's this guy?" Milt Schmidt, sitting nearby assured them that Ace would make it and that they'd get to know him.

By the 1978-79 season, Bailey was playing in the World Hockey Association for the Edmonton Oilers. It was at this time that 30-year-old Ace took a young Wayne Gretzky under his wing.

SHAWN BATES

Shawn's journey to the Bruins culminated in a virtual fairy tale experience played out on Fleet Center ice. He grew up just north of Boston in Medford and played hockey for four years at Boston University. He made the jump to the Bruins right out of his first training camp and miraculously scored a goal on his first shot in his first NHL game on October 2, 1997.

BOBBY BAUER

The name "Bauer" can be seen on the ice in every NHL game to this day, on skates and helmets. Bruins star right wing and member of the famed "Kraut Line" in the 1930s and '40s would leave his hockey career behind in 1947 while still in his prime to work in the family hockey equipment business.

One of the Bruins' fabled moments came five years after Bauer's retirement, when a night was to be held in honor of his former linemates Milt Schmidt and Woody Dumart, who were still active with the team. The decision was made to allow Bobby to come out of retirement to play a few shifts in a reunion of the "Kraut Line."

Though he was noticeably out of shape, Bauer provided a thrill for the hometown fans as he scored a goal and assisted on another before slipping back into retirement.

DICK BITTNER

Goalie Bittner made his NHL debut on February 12, 1950 at the Boston Garden, as he played the entire game in a 3-3 tie versus Detroit. Bittner had just been promoted that afternoon from the amateur Boston Olympics to replace injured Bruins goalie Jack Gelineau.

What is rather unusual is that Bittner had just shut out Atlantic City 4-0 for the Olympics that same afternoon on the same Garden ice. For all his trouble, Bittner was never given the chance to play another NHL game.

JOHN BLUE

The backup goaltender for three seasons with the Bruins in the early to mid-1990s had a background that would clearly not suggest a future in the National Hockey League. Born and brought up in Huntington Beach, California, Blue was an avid surfer, spending much of his time around water that was not frozen. His hockey journey, which began in Southern California, took him to the University of Minnesota, and after five years at the minor-league level, he made his debut with the Bruins in 1992. He recorded his only NHL goal against the Pittsburgh Penguins in his rookie season on January 14, 1993.

LEO BOIVIN

Of all the players who spent the majority of their NHL careers with the Bruins and were ultimately elected to the Hockey Hall of Fame, few have been more forgotten than Leo Boivin. The stocky defenseman, who played in the NHL right up until 1970 spent 12 seasons with Boston from 1954 to 1966.

An All-Star with the Bruins three times and the team's captain from 1963 to '66, Boivin was given the Hall of Fame honor largely because he was one of the best body checkers ever to come along. When Ted Green joined the team in the very early 1960s, it was Boivin who taught him the intimidating style of play and the finer points of body checking. Leo also worked with a young Eddie Westfall and taught him the most effective method of hip-checking.

Boivin was originally Bruins property when they traded him while he was still in the minor leagues, sending him to Toronto along with Fernie Flaman. He debuted with the Maple Leafs in 1952, but was traded back to Boston in November of 1954. For the next 12 seasons he was one of the mainstays of the Bruins' defense.

In June of 1966 Boivin was traded by Boston to Detroit for youngster Gary Doak and Ron Murphy, missing by three months the opportunity to share his wealth of knowledge with rookie Bobby Orr. Though Boivin missed being a part of the "Big Bad Bruins," he served that edition well by not only instructing players like Green and Westfall, but being instrumental in allowing the team to acquire players like Doak and Murphy.

Hall of Famer Leo Boivin may never have his uniform number 20 hanging in the Fleet Center rafters, but he deserves to have his memory brought out from the shadows.

Marcel Bonin

Bonin was a forward who came to the Bruins along with goalie Terry Sawchuk in a trade with Detroit in June of 1955, spending the 1955-56 season with Boston. He is the only known Bruin to have wrestled a real bruin—actually an eight-foot-tall brown bear.

When he was 16 years old, Barnum and Bailey's Circus came to his town, and as part of the show they offered $1,000 to anyone who could wrestle and pin the bear. Bonin lost three matches to the bear, who had no claws and wore a muzzle.

The bear certainly must have made the ruffians of the NHL seem tame by comparison.

Boston Arena

The old arena on St. Botolph Street in Boston's Back Bay was home to the team for its first four seasons until they moved into the stunning sports palace—the Boston Garden—in the fall of 1928. A trivia question has been asked on occasion over the decades that goes: "Who was the last NHL player to score a goal in the old Boston Arena?" The answer is Gordie Howe, but complicating matters is the fact that Howe wasn't born until the spring of 1928, just as the Bruins were moving out of the Arena. How can this be?

On February 25, 1952, 1,800 feet of pipes were damaged at the Boston Garden when a portion of a roof collapsed, and the Bruins-Red Wings game scheduled for the following night had to be played at the Boston Arena. The Bruins would be playing their first game back in their old home in 24 years.

Old-time Bruins star Dit Clapper was in town to visit at the time and was able to attend the game, which brought back many memories for the Hall of Famer. The ending was not a happy one for Boston fans, however, as Howe broke a 3-3 tie late in the game to give Detroit the 4-3 win. The Bruins said goodbye to the old rink once again, this time for good.

BOSTON GARDEN

The Bruins had spent their first four seasons playing in the old Boston Arena, but when the great Eddie Shore began to increase interest in the team, they quickly outgrew the old rink. Tex Rickard, who was responsible for building Madison Square Garden in New York City, was also the driving force behind the construction of Boston Garden, at a cost of $4 million. By comparison, the Fleet Center was built in the mid-1990s for $160 million. Ground was broken on December 3, 1927, and less than one year later, the building initially known as "Boston Madison Square Garden" was opened for business. Rickard had promised that the venue would be "a sports and convention center that will surpass anything of its kind in the world." The inaugural event held there was a

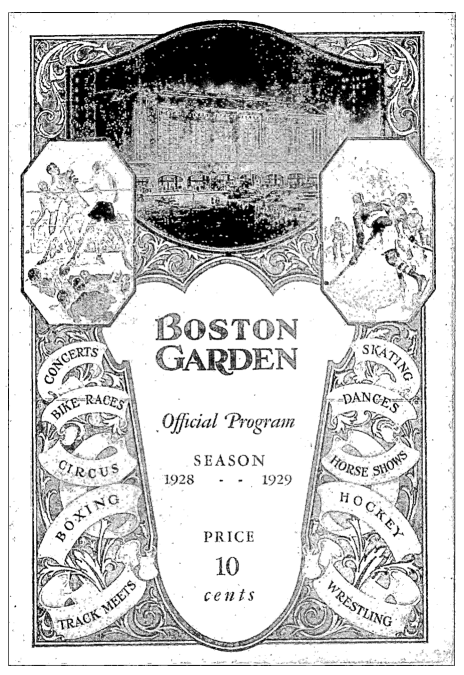

CONCERTS
BIKE RACES
CIRCUS
BOXING
TRACK MEETS

SKATING
DANCES
HORSE SHOWS
HOCKEY
WRESTLING

BOSTON GARDEN

Official Program

SEASON

1928 - - 1929

PRICE

10

cents

First program ever issued at Boston Garden upon its opening in November of 1928.

night of professional boxing on November 17, 1928, and three days later the Bruins held their first game—a 1-0 loss to the Montreal Canadiens.

In the later decades of the existence of the old Garden, there were many who attested to having sighted rodents scurrying about the building from time to time, but that seems rather run of the mill in comparison to the monkeys living up in the rafters in the 1940s.

After a circus had done a few shows in the building, they departed without realizing that a few of the monkeys had escaped and crawled up near the ceiling of the arena. The Animal Rescue League was eventually called in, and with the help of the Garden's "Bull Gang" crew, all but two of the monkeys were captured. They apparently found a hiding place, coming down when the stadium area was empty to feed on a dropped peanut, popcorn, or other morsels of food left behind. Boston sportswriter Jerry Nason wrote that he realized it was time to stop drinking when he looked up and saw a monkey peering inquisitively into the press box.

The monkeys were believed to have resided up in the rafters for approximately a year before the sightings stopped, and no one ever seemed to know what became of them.

*   *   *

The Bruins may have had a great idea, but it's just that their timing was a little off. On November 16, 1952, they held a major event at the Boston Garden that was billed as the "Silver Anniversary" of the first game they ever played at the Garden. The problem was, the 25th anniversary celebration came one year and four days too soon. The first Bruins game had been played in the Garden on November 20, 1928.

In any event, it was a terrific tribute that featured the appearances of several old-time Bruins, including Cy Denneny, George Owen, Lionel Hitchman, Cooney Weiland, Dit Clapper, Eddie Shore, and Art Ross. The old stars came out in a pregame ceremony, dressed in vintage uniforms and were all introduced to the crowd, with Eddie Shore being given the loudest ovation. The newspapers of the following day remarked jokingly that at least none of them fell down and also said it was clear that Shore had remained the most popular Bruin of all.

*   *   *

It was bad enough that the Bruins finished in last place in the NHL's American Division in the spring of 1932, but to add insult to injury they had to loan out the Boston Garden so that two other teams could play a Stanley Cup Finals game.

Madison Square Garden had become unavailable due to a circus, and the Rangers-Maple Leafs game was moved to Boston.

*   *   *

A highly unusual incident occurred at the Garden on January 15, 1934 when the ice-making machine broke down, leaving a six-foot by twelve-foot patch near one of the goal nets where there was no ice. A rubber mat was placed over the spot, and amazingly, the game between the Bruins and the St. Louis Eagles was allowed to commence. Every time the puck went to the affected area, the official would stop play.

Boston Bruins program sold at Boston Garden in the early 1950s.

Six days after the Bruins had won the Stanley Cup in 1939, the team held a formal dinner on the floor of the Boston Garden as a celebration that was attended by 1,400 fans. All of the players were in attendance, and the orchestra played the song "Paree," which was the team's theme song that was always played as they came out onto the ice before a game. Weston Adams and NHL president Frank Calder gave stirring speeches, and Eddie Shore was given an ovation every time his name was mentioned. The newspapers of the day called it an "unprecedented party."

* * *

The Bruins-Montreal game at the Garden on October 13, 1983 was noteworthy mainly because of the unusual conditions. A seemingly inexplicable fog that hovered around ice level caused action to be stopped nine times during the first period. Goalie Pete Peeters said later that Guy LeFleur came down the right side with the puck, and when he was at center ice he could only see the Canadien star's head.

Bruins radio broadcaster Bob Wilson said that the fog delays caused him to tell every hockey story he knew.

* * *

One of the last signs that the old Garden was on its last legs came in Game 4 of the 1988 Stanley Cup Finals against Edmonton on May 24 when a transformer blew, leaving the rink in total darkness. Though the lights came back on partially, the game could not be resumed and was ultimately suspended. Talk of a new arena intensified from that point on.

Ray Bourque

Three days prior to the beginning of the 1978-79 season, Harry Sinden pulled off a deal that would dramatically benefit the Bruins franchise for 20 years. He sent goaltender Ron Grahame to the Los Angeles Kings for the team's number-one draft choice in the 1979 amateur draft. Grahame had played his only NHL season to that point with the Bruins the season before, and being stuck behind goalies Gilles Gilbert and Gerry Cheevers made him expendable. The Kings' pick that the Bruins

got to make turned out to be the eighth overall pick in the 1979 draft. Boston management debated long and hard over whether they should select defenseman Keith Brown or Raymond Bourque if both were still available by the eighth pick. The Chicago Blackhawks made it fairly academic when they selected Brown, and yet the Bruins were also surprised that Bourque had fallen through the cracks and was still available and selected him.

The old Boston Garden arena in its later years.

Though Brown went on to have a 16-year career in the NHL, he didn't come close to Bourque's caliber. As for goalie Grahame, he was out of professional hockey by 1981.

*   *   *

When Bourque signed his first contract with the Bruins, he bought his father a new Oldsmobile Cutlass—in black and gold! Many forget that young Bourque was primarily French-

known as the "Big, Bad Bruins," but would come to learn that there had been many editions of such a team dating back virtually to the beginning of the franchise in the mid-1920s. When Charles Adams and Art Ross first assembled the outfit, they were in agreement that toughness would be an essential ingredient for any team that would call Boston its home.

Fans will, on occasion, feel that what is going on at that moment with the team is the most important time in its history. Yet it must be understood that each edition of the Boston Bruins hockey team is merely another link in a very long chain that stretches back to 1924, and continues on into the 21st century. Aficionados who cheer on Milan Lucic do so in the very same manner and with the same passion that Rick Middleton, John Bucyk, Fernie Flaman, Bill Cowley, Dit Clapper, and so many others from past generations were cheered on.

For so many in the New England area, rooting for the black and gold-clad warriors on ice has amounted to a lifetime commitment.

speaking at this time. Shortly after, when Raymond reported to his first Bruins training camp in Fitchburg in September of 1979, team captain Wayne Cashman knew there was something special about him—a certain charisma, and also that he simply loved to play hockey. Said Cashman: "It was like he was a Bruin all his life."

Bourque was issued uniform number 29 in training camp, but come opening night of the regular season, though he never asked for it, number seven was hanging in his stall in the Bruins locker room at Boston Garden. The team management felt it was okay to give out Phil Esposito's old number, because Phil had been a member of the Rangers for four seasons and was still active.

Ray went out that night and scored the first of his 410 career goals in a 4-0 win over the Winnipeg Jets. Not a terribly picturesque goal as it deflected off two skates, Bourque himself remembered, "It was one of the ugliest I ever scored." Adding a Hall of Fame touch to the goal was the fact that the classy Jean Ratelle had helped to set it up. It should also be noted that Bourque received credit for his first assist 40 seconds into his first shift that night.

Bourque went on in that terrific rookie season to be the only non-goalie to win both the Calder Trophy as Rookie of the Year and to be named to the first-team All-Star team. The following season in the Bruins 1980-81 game program, Boston hockey writer Joe Gordon wrote prophetically, "Barring the unforeseen, Bourque can play in this league for 20 years. Imagine having him in the lineup until the year 2000."

Raymond had a unique ritual of tapping the goalie's pads with his stick a certain way before every game, which began very early in his career when goalie Marco Baron asked him to do so. He continued to perform the ritual no matter who was in goal for the Bruins for the rest of his time with the team.

First, he would go directly in front of the goalie and tap the blocker, then the glove, then a tap on each pad, followed by a gentle tug of the blade under the goalie's crotch. He would then do a spin and then hit the glove again, then skate a quick circle followed by another tap. It was very important that no one come near either Bourque or the goalie during the procedure. Who says athletes are superstitious?

*   *   *

Few who witnessed the event will ever forget it, least of all Phil Esposito. It was December 3, 1987, and the Bruins were going to raise Esposito's number seven to the Boston Garden rafters, despite the fact that Bourque was still using it. Coach Terry O'Reilly and Harry Sinden called Bourque in that afternoon, and it was then that it was decided that Bourque would switch to number 77, though it was kept a secret from virtually everyone. When the ceremony was taking place, Bourque skated over to Phil, who didn't realize what was about to happen. Ray then peeled off his old number seven jersey, revealing his new number 77 to a shocked Esposito and an equally shocked Garden crowd.

Overlooked when the evening is recalled is the fact that the Bruins entered the third period of the game down 4-1 to one of Espo's other teams, the Rangers, but came back with three goals in the third to win 4-3. The new number 77, Bourque, added one of the three goals in the great comeback.

Raymond Bourque posed on Boston Garden ice in the late 1980s.

*   *   *

Bourque's physical conditioning is legendary, and in the early 1990s he went through a stress test at a Boston hospital. As the treadmill gradually inclined and sped up, he was able to increase his pace to a remarkable degree. The doctor in attendance said that Ray had come as close to breaking the machine as anyone had.

Bourque was always able to log an incredible amount of minutes, between 30 and 35 per game. Harry Sinden said near the end of Ray's career, "As he got older, the minutes he played didn't decline, they increased!" In the playoff game against Carolina that went into triple overtime, Bourque played nearly 45 minutes. The following day he reported for practice, ready to go out on the ice, even though he was so stiff he could barely bend over to put his skates on. Coach Pat Burns tried to convince him that he didn't have to go out, but Ray insisted. Burns and all of the players present were awed by his love of the game and the leadership he showed.

In a game at the Fleet Center in 1999, Bourque got in the way of a slapshot off the stick of the Kings' Ray Ferraro and had four of his front teeth knocked out. He went back to the dressing room to be treated, and thinking, "It was only teeth," he practically begged the doctor to let him go back into the game, but it was felt that the gash was just too deep.

*   *   *

Late in his career, Bourque became involved in a charity auction to benefit the family of a young man who had died unexpectedly, leaving a wife and four children behind. The man's son had played youth hockey with Ray's son, and Ray convinced several star athletes to get involved and to donate items to be auctioned off for the cause. Ray himself contributed one of his own game-worn jerseys, which was the final item up for bid at the auction.

Ray himself started the bidding, and as things progressed, several bids had driven the price up. A while later, a voice from the back of the room called out "$5,000," and everyone was surprised when they realized it was the voice of Bourque. It was quickly made official that his was the winning bid, and Ray walked up front to get the jersey and immediately took it over to the family and presented it to the children.

No one who knew Ray Bourque well was terribly surprised by the act of kindness.

For each game, the Bruins order 24 hockey sticks for Bourque. On the morning of the game, he inspects the sticks, picking out four to be available for the game. The rest are given away as souvenirs or donated to charities to be auctioned off.

Bourque uses five different pairs of hockey gloves during the course of a game, rotating between the five so that he will always be using a dry pair.

NICK BOYNTON

When the defenseman from Etobicoke, Ontario, came to his first Bruins training camp, he was desperately trying to make the team, but ran up against an unexpected physical challenge. He noticed that he was thirsty all of the time and constantly fatigued, but when he realized that he had lost 20 pounds, it became obvious that tests needed to be done. When the results came back, it had been discovered that he had Type One diabetes, which really knocked him for a loop. Boynton experienced a range of emotions, and questioned whether or not he would be able to achieve his dream of playing in the NHL.

Nick quickly educated himself about the condition, and in a short time he was able to keep it under control while maintaining the conditioning required for the NHL. Road roommate Hal Gill may have been a bit squeamish when he first observed Boynton injecting himself with insulin, but he learned to take it all in stride. Boynton even took to visiting a local diabetes clinic and talking to young patients afflicted with the condition.

FRANKIE BRIMSEK

The circumstances surrounding Brimsek's promotion to the Bruins caused an uproar among the team and its fans. Brought up from the Providence farm team in late November of 1938, the 22-year-old goalie from Minnesota would be replacing a Boston hockey legend. Cecil "Tiny" Thompson had just been traded to Detroit to make way for Brimsek, and it reigned as the biggest shock on the Boston sports scene since Babe Ruth was sold to the Yankees nearly two decades prior. Coach and general manager Art Ross defended the trade, say-

*Frankie Brimsek—"Mr. Zero"—in his
final season with the Boston Bruins.*

ing that he felt that Brimsek had a chance to be even better
than the great Thompson, and the $15,000 they received for
him would help to purchase and develop more young players. Bruins players were furious with the sale of Thompson,
and his roommate Dit Clapper blasted the team, saying they
may as well trade him also. After meeting with Ross, Clapper
recanted his statements.

Thompson and Ross had actually been at odds since
1932. That year, Ross had tried out goalies Wilf Cude and
Percy Jackson, as Thompson left the team for a short time.
Bruins management announced that he had gone away to rest

in order to avoid a "nervous breakdown," and Tiny greatly resented the implication. The relationship between Ross and Thompson had been strained since that time. With Detroit, Thompson was never a major force in goal again, and was out of the league in less than two seasons.

Ross timed the move so that Brimsek would play his first two games on the road. In his first game with Boston on December 1, 1938, Frankie's debut was spoiled as he allowed two goals to the Canadiens in Montreal's 2-0 win. Then moving on to Chicago, he managed to record a shutout as the Bruins won 5-0, setting the stage for his Boston Garden debut on December 6.

The Boston Garden crowd, which usually cheered the Bruins wildly as they came out on to the ice were strangely quiet, undoubtedly somewhat resentful of the young goalie wearing Thompson's No. 1 on his Boston sweater. But when he skated off the Garden ice after 60 minutes of hockey with a 2-0 victory, he had won their hearts. In the next game five days later in New York, he managed yet another shutout, a 3-0 win over the Rangers. Two days later with Montreal in town, Brimsek and the Bruins hung on for a 3-2 win, but he had surpassed Thompson's scoreless record of 224 minutes by seven minutes before finally letting in a goal.

Frankie then went on another streak in which he recorded three more consecutive shutouts, which amounted to six shutouts in his first seven games. In the *Boston Post* of December 20, 1938, Arthur Duffey wrote, "The Bruins are hot, and Frankie Brimsek is perhaps the hottest of them all. He's making the fans forget Tiny Thompson."

"Mr. Zero" was born.

Ross Brooks

Brooks attended his first Bruins training camp in 1958, and after paying his dues for 14 minor-league seasons, the goaltender finally got his chance in the NHL with Boston at the age of 35 during the 1972-73 season. He had been released by Providence in early 1971, and desperately trying to keep his career alive, sent letters to nearly every pro team he could think of for a tryout. The Bruins took him up on it and assigned him to their Oklahoma City farm team. Being promoted for a trial with Boston in 1972-73 he became the first Jewish Bruins goalie since Moe Roberts in the 1920s. The following season he equaled Bruins legend Tiny Thompson's NHL record of 14 straight wins. Unfortunately, Brooks could not sustain his level of play, and with the presence of Gilles Gilbert and the return of Gerry Cheevers, there was little chance for him, and he was out of hockey after the 1975-76 season.

Johnny Bucyk

As a youth playing hockey on the frozen ponds of Alberta, Canada, Bucyk and his pals would often use frozen pieces of horse manure as pucks when an actual rubber puck wasn't available. As the story goes, he would follow a horse-drawn milk wagon to school, and when the horse stopped and left his droppings, Johnny would stick them in a snow bank to freeze, and come back after school to pick them up.

Later, when Johnny was playing junior hockey for the Edmonton Oil Kings, his coach thought he skated so poorly he made him take figure skating lessons in order to improve. He made it up to the NHL with the Detroit Red Wings during the 1955-56 season, and his first fight, a stick fight, came in Boston Garden versus Bruins defenseman Jack Bionda. The two combatants would be teammates the following season after Bucyk's trade to the Bruins. Johnny's first fight as a member of the Bruins came against Claude LaForge of his old team, the Red Wings, whom he pummeled. Bucyk was a player who liked a rough, tough style of hockey, but really didn't care for fighting. It only took him manhandling a few opponents who challenged him early in his career to drastically reduce the number of opponents who dared. Johnny was capable of delivering devastating but clean body checks, and the fact that he was able to routinely dish out such punishment yet still win the Lady Byng Trophy twice is a testament to his cleanliness and sportsmanship.

*   *   *

When Bucyk came to the Bruins in a trade that sent future Hall of Fame goalie Terry Sawchuk to Detroit, he was reunited with Bronco Horvath and Vic Stasiuk, former linemates from the Edmonton Flyers in the Western Hockey League in 1953. Bucyk, who became known as "the Chief" had no Indian blood whatsoever, but was 100 percent Ukranian. It was linemate Horvath who had given him the nickname. Thought to be all Ukranian, Bucyk, Horvath and Stasiuk were dubbed "the 'Uke' line." Horvath, however, was all Hungarian, but he didn't object to the line's nickname. The linemates not only worked together with the Bruins, they lived together as well, renting a house in nearby Arlington.

Boston made it to the Stanley Cup Finals in Bucyk's first season with the team, but would not get back there for 12 years. He would come to think of the Bruins' eight-season playoff drought from 1961 through 1967 as "the dark days." His first Stanley Cup Championship came in his 15th season. A big change for him came in training camp in September of 1967. When Bruins left wing Ross Lonsberry was injured, new coach Sinden put Bucyk on a line with newly acquired center Fred Stanfield and right wing Johnny McKenzie, and the line was extremely successful in its five seasons together.

* * *

When Bucyk first came to the Bruins, he started a habit of being the last Bruin out on the ice from the dressing room. He continued this habit right up into the 1970s.

On December 10, 1970, Bucyk appeared in his 1,000[th] NHL game, and was honored by the Bruins in a pregame ceremony as team president Weston Adams Jr. presented him with a $1,000 bill. In the 8-2 win over Buffalo, Bucyk scored two goals and had four assists as the Bruins assaulted the Sabres with 72 shots on goal.

* * *

Johnny Bucyk in the early years of his 21-season career with Boston. The "Chief" was given his nickname around this time by fellow linemate Bronco Horvath.

When the Bruins won the Stanley Cup in 1972, the clinching game occurred the evening before Bucyk's 37th birthday. As the locker room celebration was carrying on for some time, one of his teammates looked at the clock and noticed it had turned to midnight, and they all joined in to sing "Happy Birthday" to Johnny.

Pat Burns

The former coach of the Bruins, Maple Leafs, and Canadiens grew up in Montreal with a father who didn't speak French and mother who didn't speak English. Burns was showing a fondness for the Bruins at an early age. Wearing the Bruins sweater around his Montreal neighborhood caused him to be in fights both on and off the ice. He never played at a level higher than junior hockey, and ended up serving as a police officer for 17 years. It was Wayne Gretzky who talked him into coaching at the junior hockey level, and within a little more than a decade, the guitar-playing, Harley-riding coach had held a few of the most-coveted hockey jobs in North America.

Lyndon Byers

Born on Leap Day of 1964, Lyndon was a fun-loving, rambunctious Bruin who was popular with the hometown fans and rarely passed up an opportunity to trade punches with the opposition. After nine seasons with the Bruins organization, with very few dull moments along the way, L.B. signed with the San Jose Sharks on November 7, 1992 for what would be his final NHL season.

Byers came back to the Boston Garden for the first time in an opposing uniform on January 18, 1993, flying his father in for the game and also supplying tickets for 50 friends. It was an eventful evening for Lyndon as he scored what would be his last NHL goal that game, coming off Andy Moog.

JIM CAREY

A local boy who grew up in the Boston suburb of Weymouth, Carey was acquired by the Bruins the season after he won the Vezina Trophy as the NHL's best goalie with the Washington Capitals. His first game with Boston was at the Fleet Center on March 3, 1997, two days after the trade, but it turned out to be a disaster in front of family and friends.

Carey allowed four goals to Toronto in the first period and was pulled by coach Steve Kasper before the start of the second period. Rob Tallas came on and allowed no goals in the final two periods. Someone asked Carey jokingly after the game if he'd "like to take a mulligan."

In the next Bruins game three days later, things did not get a whole lot better as Carey was in net for a 5-2 loss to the Islanders in New York. But he redeemed himself at least in some small way two days later. This time it was Tallas who started and allowed four goals in the first period. Carey was inserted in net to start the second period, and shut Tampa Bay out the rest of the game in the Bruins' 6-4 win.

Carey's time in Boston turned out to be terribly disappointing overall. In the fall of 1998 he was unable to beat out Byron Dafoe for the starting job and was sent down to Providence of the AHL. The following season he hooked on with the St. Louis Blues.

WAYNE CARLETON

Left wing "Swoop" Carleton may best be remembered in his time with the Bruins for being on the ice when Bobby Orr scored his famous goal to win the Stanley Cup in 1970. Wayne, number 11, was one of the first to get to Orr to congratulate him after ending the series.

In the summer of 1971, Carleton was claimed by the California Seals in the Intra-League draft. In a game against the Bruins the following February, the Seals had a 5-2 lead after the second period, and Wayne teased a few of his former teammates that they had them beat.

Boston came back and won the game 8-6.

WAYNE CASHMAN

Cashman spent 16 seasons in the NHL, all with Boston, and earned several noteworthy distinctions. He served as the Bruins' captain for his last six seasons, concluding his career after the 1982-83 season. During that final campaign, he was the last NHL player to remain from the old six-team league of 1966-67. He was also regarded by many to have had the best

Only five Bruins have scored more points than the rugged left winger. "Cash" was keeping the spirit of the "Big, Bad Bruins" of the '60s and '70s alive in the 21st century as an assistant coach for the team.

left hook in the league. Likely his finest individual performance didn't come until his 11th season in the league at nearly 33 years old. On April 2, 1978, he scored four goals against his old linemates Phil Esposito and Ken Hodge's New York Rangers.

When Esposito had been traded to New York back in early November of 1975, Cashman was deeply affected and let his emotions get the best of him. The night the team was informed of the deal while in Vancouver, Espo's former left wing started to take it out on his hotel room. By the time he was finished, the room looked like a bomb had exploded in it.

Shortly after, Cashman wrote out a hefty check to the hotel to pay for the considerable damage.

One of the most popular tales involving Wayne Cashman occurred in the early 1970s when he had been taken into custody by police in Massachusetts for a motor vehicle violation. When he was taken back to the station, he was allowed one phone call according to his Miranda rights.

Rather than calling his attorney, he called a local Chinese restaurant, and a short time later a large quantity of food was delivered to the police station.

CHANNEL 38—WSBK BOSTON

It is channel 38, one of Boston's early UHF television stations, which started broadcasting Bruins games in the fall of 1967 that deserves a portion of the credit for dramatically increasing the team's popularity. Nearly everyone who was a regular viewer in the early years can hum the opening theme song, yet few remember that the title of the ditty was "Nut Rocker."

Station general manager William Flynn, who had just taken over the position early in 1967 offered a television contract to both the Boston Celtics and Bruins. The Celtics declined the offer, but the Bruins began a relationship with channel 38 that would last 35 years. One reason that Bruins president Weston Adams Sr. accepted the offer was that he would now be able to watch virtually every Bruins game on the road while he was back at home in the Boston area.

At first, 38 televised only Bruins road games, but a severe snowstorm in Boston paved the way for a significant change in philosophy. On the day of the storm, Adams was afraid that fans wouldn't be able to make it to the Garden that night for the game and asked Flynn if he would deviate from the contract and televise it as a favor to those fans. As it turned out, all of the fans were able to make it to the game and the Garden was full, but they still drew a terrific television audience. This demonstrated to them that televising home games might not hurt attendance after all, and games from Boston Garden became available to the local viewers shortly after.

GERRY CHEEVERS

Cheevers had made his NHL debut in December of 1961 with the Toronto Maple Leafs, having been called up for a couple of games to replace the injured Johnny Bower. He went back down and spent the next few seasons in Toronto's minor league system. In June of 1965, the Leafs had a dilemma with the upcoming intra-league draft. They had three goalies that they wanted to protect, Bower, Terry Sawchuk, and

Cheevers, but could only protect two. They thought they had found a rather sneaky solution when they decided to protect Cheevers as a forward. Their rather questionable reasoning was that Cheevers had played forward for a few games in juniors several years before. When league officials noticed the tactic, they disallowed it, and the Bruins were able to draft him for the $30,000 fee.

Cheevers's career with Boston got off to a somewhat rocky start. On December 2, 1965 he appeared in his second game in goal with the Bruins, and they were soundly thrashed by the Red Wings 10-2. After the game, Bruins general manager Hap Emms stormed into the team's dressing room and insisted on an explanation for what happened. Cheevers summed it up simply, "Roses are red, violets are blue, they got ten and we got two!" This did not endear young Cheevers to the straight-laced Emms.

Considered one of the great "money" goalies, "Cheesy" showed on at least one occasion that intense preparation is not always 100 percent necessary. In the playoffs in April of 1979 against Pittsburgh, Cheevers had won the first two games, and Coach Cherry decided to start Gilles Gilbert in game three at Pittsburgh. Just prior to the start of the game, Gilbert came down with a case of hives and was unable to play. Cheevers had eaten two hot dogs and washed it down with two sodas just before Cherry told him he would have to start, but he went out and had a great game, winning 2-1.

*   *   *

A young Gerry Cheevers in his early years in Boston before he donned his famous mask.

Cheevers's goalie mask featuring stitches all over it quickly became his trademark. Debuting in the NHL with the Bruins on October 27, 1965, he went on to play his first two seasons without a mask, but on opening night of the 1967-68 season, he had adopted one permanently. Shortly after, he had taken a hard shot off the forehead and realized that without the mask he would have needed several stitches. Assistant trainer John Forristall painted the approximate amount of stitches Cheevers would have received on the forehead of the mask, and the tradition was born.

Cheevers was an intense competitor and never went along with the tradition of shaking his opponents' hands after the conclusion of a playoff series. At the end of the 1972 Stanley Cup final victory over the Rangers, he extended his disdain for the opposition further to include their fans. The New York fans had been brutal towards Bruins players, and Cheevers was even hit in the head with a bag of peanuts. After time had expired at Madison Square Garden on May 11, 1972 and the Bruins had won game six to win the Cup, Cheevers shouted to the crowd repeatedly "Eat your hearts out!"

*　　*　　*

Cheevers had signed with the new World Hockey Association's Cleveland Crusaders shortly after the Bruins had won the Stanley Cup in 1972. After two and a half seasons he had had enough. He left the Cleveland team, and finally convinced them to release him from his contract. Cheevers then returned to the Bruins in grand fashion.

In his first game back with the team on February 8, 1976, he shut out the Detroit Red Wings by the lopsided score of 7-0. Hockey fan Henry Kissinger was among the lucky Garden patrons who witnessed Cheevers's return.

*　　*　　*

In December of 1978, longtime teammate Wayne Cashman raved about Cheevers to Francis Rosa of the *Boston Globe*, saying, "Next to Bobby Orr, he's the greatest player ever. He takes control of the game. Think what that means, a goalie controlling the game! But he does. He does it with his handling of the puck and by talking all the time. He keeps reminding us where to go, and you do what he says because that gives him an outlet for the puck."

Such comments illustrate why Cheevers was one of the very few ex-goaltenders to become a coach in the NHL. Legendary Russian goalie Vladislav Tretiak was also quoted as saying that Cheevers was the greatest goaltender he had ever seen.

* * *

Phil Esposito said of his friend Cheevers that he loved horses so much, if there is such a thing as reincarnation, the goalie wants to come back as a horse. He bought his first racehorse, Cenacle's Image, in the spring of 1970, and by 1976, his horse Royal Ski was the leading money winner among two-year-olds that year finishing ahead of the legendary Seattle Slew. He was beginning to make good on his intention to recoup some of the money he had lost at racetracks over the years.

* * *

Very late in his career, he had just returned from a knee injury and was taken out of the game after giving up seven goals. After the game a reporter said to him, "You looked a little slow getting up after some of those shots." Cheevers responded dryly, "Actually, there was no rush. They were just getting back to center ice to face off."

*Gerry Cheevers, sporting the mask that would make him
one of the most recognizable goalies in NHL history.*

When Cheevers was hired as coach of the Bruins on July 7, 1980, Ray Fitzgerald of the *Boston Globe* asked him about his relationship with the players, many of whom had been his teammates. He replied, "If I walk into a bar and four Bruins were sitting there, I don't want them to scatter just because the coach has shown up. I want to sit down and have a beer with them, same as always... especially if they pick up the check!"

Also, shortly after he was hired he was asked by Bruins public relations director Nate Greenberg to do a radio interview. Cheevers shot back, "For crying out loud, Nate, I've been a coach for ten minutes, and you're already a pain in the butt." Gerry had long been thought of as the "Don Rickles" of the Bruins, as he was constantly needling his teammates.

* * *

When asked in an interview in the early 1970s which NHL team gave him the most trouble, Cheevers deadpanned "The Bruins!"

DON CHERRY

While "Grapes," as Don Cherry was known became a popular and notoriously outspoken coach for the Bruins in the 1970s, his NHL playing career was over almost before it began. The defenseman out of Kingston, Ontario, born on the same day as baseball great Hank Aaron (2/5/34) worked his way through the Bruins system quickly and appeared in one game for Boston (wearing the now-famous number 24)

Don Cherry, upon being hired as coach of the Bruins in 1974.

during the playoffs after the 1954-55 regular season. That summer, he hurt his shoulder playing baseball, and while he would spend 15 more seasons toiling at the minor-league level, he never played another game in the NHL.

Cherry nearly always had comments that would raise an eyebrow. When he was hired to coach the Bruins in June of 1974, a reporter asked about a situation when he was coaching Rochester of the AHL where he reportedly got into a physical confrontation with one of his players. "Aw, it wasn't a fistfight," he snapped. "I just grabbed a loafing player by the shirt and shook him a bit. Yes, it had the desired effect."

In his first season coaching the Bruins, Chicago's Stan Makita had engaged in a bit of treacherous stick work on Bobby Orr, and Cherry wailed afterwards, "If he does that again, he'll get sent back to Czechoslovakia in a box!"

The comment was thought by many to be in rather questionable taste, and Cherry was encouraged to apologize for the remark.

Cherry often had colorful and controversial comments aimed at NHL on-ice officials. Bruce Hood was understandably offended when Cherry said that anyone interested should bet on the opposition any time Hood worked a Boston game.

After a 3-2 loss to Cleveland in 1978, Cherry raised more eyebrows when he said, "I definitely believe the referees have orders, or they sit down and have a few beers together and decide. The referees control this league. They control the scores. I definitely feel the referees have orders to get the Boston Bruins."

CHRISTMAS NIGHT BRAWLS
AT THE GARDEN

The Bruins have, on occasion, had a nice way of celebrating Christmas on Boston Garden ice. The notion of "peace on earth and goodwill toward men" has been set aside once every several decades.

On December 25, 1930, the Bruins were hosting the Philadelphia Quakers for a little post-holiday dinner hockey, but the Quakers clearly did not adhere to the peace-loving philosophy that their name would imply. The two teams became embroiled in a battle that became so out of control, the Boston police had to intervene and considered calling in the marines from a nearby base for reinforcements. It should be no surprise that Eddie Shore was in the middle of it all.

Thirty-seven years later on Christmas night of 1967, the expansion Oakland Seals were making only their second appearance in Boston when things turned ugly. Seals coach Bert Olmstead left the bench to confront an unruly fan, and a donnybrook ensued, making for yet another memorable Christmas on ice.

DIT CLAPPER

Clapper holds a unique distinction in Bruins history in that he is the only player to have played on three Boston Stanley Cup-winning teams, doing so in 1929, 1939, and 1941. His career was also unique for having played right wing for his first 11 seasons, and switched to defense full time for his final nine seasons, making the All-Star team at both positions. Also, by playing in the 1946-47 season, Clapper became the first NHL player to play 20 seasons. When he decided to retire as an active player in February of 1947, he was immediately put into the Hockey Hall of Fame, the only player so honored. An elaborate ceremony was held at the Boston Garden the night of his last game, February 12, 1947, and he presented his famous No. 5 Bruins sweater to the Hall of Fame right there on the spot.

Though Dit was a clean and gentlemanly player, he was recognized by his peers as the best boxer in the league. In the late 1920s, the Canadian Heavyweight Boxing Champion was

"Tiny" Thompson (left) and Cooney Weiland were longtime teammates of Dit Clapper.

Lionel Conacher, and many players felt that Clapper could have beaten him in a boxing ring. They marveled at Dit as a physical specimen. One night in a brawl against Ottawa, three players came at Clapper in succession and he knocked each one down with one punch—three right in a row.

* * *

Clapper took over for Ross as the Bruins coach beginning with the 1945-46 season, serving as player-coach until February of 1947, then coached in street clothes until the end of the 1948-49 season. After the end of that season, he made

43

the surprising announcement at a team dinner that he was stepping down as coach. He said, "To be a really good coach you have to drive the guys. I couldn't really do that, because I like them too much." Clapper was just 42 years old and probably could have coached the team, or at least worked in the organization for as long as he wanted, but he walked away from hockey for good.

ROY CONACHER

As a teenager in the early 1930s, Toronto-native Conacher worked selling programs during hockey games at Maple Leaf Gardens. By 1938 the left winger had made his NHL debut with the Bruins, and immediately made a name for himself by leading the league in goals. Boston made it to the Stanley Cup finals at the end of Conacher's rookie season, and the former program hawker scored several goals against his hometown Leafs to help capture the Bruins' second Lord Stanley trophy.

BILLY COUTU

The brutal defenseman nicknamed "Wild" Billy came to the Bruins in a trade with the Montreal Canadiens before the 1926-27 season. He is remembered for a collision in his first training camp with Boston in which young Eddie Shore almost lost his ear. In the Stanley Cup Finals against the old Ottawa Senators the following spring, coach Art Ross was so infuriated by what he felt was horrible officiating, he reportedly

*Bill Cowley, one of the league's great playmakers,
won the MVP Award in 1941 and 1943.*

offered a $500 reward for physical retribution on a certain referee. Accepting the offer, Coutu chased the official down and pummeled him, and is believed to have collected the bounty.

A week later, Coutu was suspended from the NHL for life for the incident.

BILL COWLEY

The outstanding center from the late 1930s and '40s tended to be a bit overshadowed by Milt Schmidt and the "Kraut Line," but was recognized enough to receive the Hart

Trophy in 1941 and 1943 as well as the first-team All-Star team in 1938, 1941, 1943, and 1944. At the time of his retirement in 1947 he was actually the NHL's all-time leader in both assists and points.

The extremely smooth and accurate passing center was said to have "made more wings than Boeing."

JACK CRAWFORD

The fine defenseman spent his entire career with Boston from 1937 to 1950, and was part of two Stanley Cup champion Bruins teams in 1939 and 1941. He was one of the very few players during that time to wear a helmet, but may have had a bit of extra incentive to protect his head.

He was rather embarrassed by the fact that he was almost completely bald and his helmet tended to conceal that fact.

FRED CUSICK

The Boston broadcasting legend retired from calling Bruins hockey games in 1997 after a stellar 45-year career that began in 1952 shortly after serving in the Korean War. But Fred's interest in hockey was not strictly relegated to being behind the microphone. He had played for Boston University in the late 1930s and early '40s and had been a teammate there of forward Ed Barry, who went on to play briefly with the Bruins in 1946-47.

On January 26, 1957, Cusick announced the first Bruins game ever televised nationally in the United States as Boston hosted the Rangers at the Garden on CBS television. Fred was still broadcasting the occasional minor-league hockey game as recently as early 2003 at the age of 83.

BYRON DAFOE

The star goaltender was born in the unlikely location of Sussex, England. He was given a name befitting his nativity, being named after the 19th century poet Lord Byron. Dafoe can likely thank Gerry Cheevers for him being acquired by the Bruins in 1997. Cheevers had watched a minor-league game in Baltimore in 1993 and saw Dafoe tending goal for that city's Skipjacks of the American Hockey League. He went back and recommended the young goalie to Harry Sinden, who kept him in mind and followed his progress until he had the chance to trade for him before the 1997-98 season.

NICK DAMORE

The Damore family of Niagara Falls, Ontario, may question whether or not they received ample opportunity to prove themselves in the NHL. Goalie Nick Damore, who had toiled for several seasons at the minor-league level, was finally called up to the Bruins on January 25, 1942. The team's star goalie Frankie Brimsek had broken his nose after appearing in 194 straight games.

Damore got the start against Montreal and beat the Canadiens 7-3 at the Garden. Unfortunately for Damore, Brimsek came back the next game and Damore was promptly sent back to Hershey, never getting another chance to appear in an NHL game.

Damore's brother Hank, a forward, also spent numerous years in junior and minor-league hockey, but his NHL career consisted of four games with the New York Rangers in the 1943-44 season.

Cy Denneny

Old Cy occupies a special place in Boston Bruins lore. In the fall of 1928, just as the Boston Garden was ready to make its debut, Bruins coach Art Ross decided to step away from coaching temporarily in order to concentrate on general manager duties. Three weeks before the 1928-29 season was to begin, he bought veteran star left winger Denneny from the old Ottawa Senators and appointed him player-coach of the team. Cy went on to lead the Bruins that season to their first Stanley Cup, christening the new Boston Garden with a championship in its inaugural season. The Cup-clinching game occurred in New York against the Rangers, and Cy carried the Cup off the ice after the game and put it in the upper berth of a Pullman Sleeper car for the joyous trip back to Boston. Denneny had played his last game of professional hockey and had gone out on a terrific note.

Denneny claimed years later to be the first player to use a curved blade on his hockey stick, though no other player at that time picked up on the trend. Decades later, Blackhawk Stan Mikita adopted it, and it then became the rage.

Though he didn't pioneer the trend among his peers, Cy did well for himself with the stick. When he retired from the game, he was the NHL career leader in goals scored.

GARY DOAK

The popular defenseman served two tours of duty with the Bruins during his 16-season NHL career. After being lost in the expansion draft of 1970 to the new Vancouver Canucks, Gary spent time also with the Rangers and Red Wings before returning to Boston late in the 1972-73 season.

Doak was pretty strictly a defensive defenseman, and made a surprise contribution on January 30, 1976 with his first NHL goal in five seasons. The goal was the game-winner in the Bruins' 4-2 win over the Atlanta Flames. Making it seem all the more unlikely was the fact that Gary had a broken wrist that was being held together with a stiff leather brace.

His Boston teammates gave him a considerable razzing afterwards for his offensive "explosion."

*   *   *

On opening night of the 1977-78 season, Doak had his front teeth chipped by the stick of Atlanta's Harold Philipoff. The generally mild-mannered Bruins defenseman retaliated with a cross-check that got him sent to the penalty box, which resulted in a power-play goal for Atlanta.

When asked about his actions by a reporter after the game he responded, "When you get something like that, you don't shake hands with the guy."

PAT EGAN

A fine defenseman for the Bruins from 1944 to 1949, the burly, brawling Egan has the distinction of having worn both Eddie Shore's No. 2 and Bobby Orr's No. 4 during his six-season stint with the team. He was acquired by coach Art Ross in an attempt to find the next Eddie Shore—an attempt that has arguably been unsuccessful to this day.

PHIL ESPOSITO

In the spring of 1967, Chicago Blackhawks general manager Tommy Ivan had become disillusioned with his underachieving 25-year-old center Phil Esposito. Just before NHL teams were required to freeze their rosters for the upcoming expansion draft with which the league would stock six brand new teams, Chicago and Boston agreed to a trade that included Esposito. Some observers believed that if Esposito had not been traded, he almost surely would have been left unprotected in the draft and been chosen by one of the new teams. It is extremely difficult to imagine Esposito spending time in the late 1960s as a member of the Oakland Seals, or some other collection of newly formed team of castoffs. Bruins general manager Milt Schmidt, who had just taken over, saw Phil's potential, and by acquiring him, Ken Hodge and Fred Stanfield made what is still regarded as one of the most lopsided deals in the history of the league. In Boston it became known as the biggest heist since the Brinks job. While the Blackhawks received three players, Pit Martin, Gilles Marotte, and Jack Norris, who went on to be clearly less accomplished players, the Bruins received three players who were a large part of two Stanley Cup champions.

When Phil came to the Bruins he was in the final year of a contract that would pay him $18,500 for the year, but Schmidt immediately gave him a $4,000 raise, which made him feel wanted. When he reported to his first Boston training camp he gave a spirited pep talk to his new teammates, predicting that the team, which had finished in last place the season before would rise up steadily in the standings. He also stated prophetically that they would win the Stanley Cup by 1970.

It didn't take long for the Blackhawks to realize they made a mistake in letting Phil go. In December of 1967, his first season with Boston, he scored a hat trick against his old team in a 7-2 win.

*   *   *

Phil faced his goaltender brother, Tony, for the first time in the NHL on December 5, 1968, shortly after he had been brought up by the Canadiens. The rookie goalie had made his debut six days earlier in Oakland when he had come on

Phil Esposito in 1974.

in relief of starter Rogie Vachon. The game against the Bruins in the Garden was to be his first NHL start.

The good news for young Tony was that he managed to come away with a respectable 2-2 tie on the road against the tough Bruins. The bad news was that both goals scored against him were scored by big brother Phil. Eight minutes into the first period, Phil took a pass from Ted Green and shot it past Tony. About midway through the third period, Bobby Orr passed it to Phil, who let a slapshot rip, beating Tony again. Phil received a call from his mother after the game, and she was none too pleased. Phil behaved better in his next game against his brother. The two met again two and a half weeks later in Montreal, and the result was a 0-0 tie.

Phil and Tony met in the second round of the playoffs in the spring of 1970, with the goalie now playing for Phil's old team, the Blackhawks. It was the first time in the NHL in 41 years that a goaltender would be facing his brother in the playoffs since the Bruins' Tiny Thompson faced his brother Paul of the Rangers. In the first game, Phil scored three goals on Tony in a 6-3 win.

*   *   *

When Espo first came to the Bruins, he dressed in the stall next to Johnny Bucyk. Just as Phil would pull his jersey over his head, Bucyk would undo his suspenders without him knowing about it. When Phil then left the dressing room to go out to the ice to skate around in warmups, his hockey pants would fall down. He pulled this stunt several times, and everyone on the team knew it except Phil, who finally caught on.

*   *   *

After the Bruins' elimination from the Stanley Cup playoffs in April of 1973, the team scheduled a breakup party to say goodbye for the summer. Phil had missed the last few weeks due to a knee operation and was recuperating in a Boston hospital.

Several of his teammates snuck into Massachussetts General Hospital and wheeled Phil in his hospital bed out to the nearby "Branding Iron" restaurant, partly owned by Bobby Orr, where the party was being held. A couple of the players reportedly removed a door at the hospital from its hinges in order to get the bed out.

*   *   *

On November 7, 1975, coach Don Cherry had the task of informing Esposito that he had been traded to the Rangers. The team was on the road in Vancouver, and Cherry called him to his hotel room and told him he had been traded. Before he told him which team he would be going to, Phil said, "Please tell me they traded me to any team but the Rangers." As soon as Cherry confirmed the worst, Phil started crying.

EUROPEAN TOUR—1959

One seemingly forgotten incident in Bruins history is the Bruins-Rangers exhibition tour of Europe a few weeks after the conclusion of the 1958-59 season. A Swiss promoter had arranged the barnstorming tour, hoping to spread interest in the game at the professional level. Rinks and leagues were starting to sprout up all over the continent, and two NHL teams promised to be quite a show. Each player was to be paid $1,000, along with receiving gifts such as luggage and watches.

Most of the players had never been to Europe and were excited about the prospect. John Bucyk, Fernie Flaman, Leo Labine, Fleming Mackell, and Don Simmons were a few of the more prominent players representing the Bruins. The Rangers, short a couple of players to take over, borrowed a young Bobby Hull to accompany them. The 20-year-old Hull had just finished his second season with Chicago, but would now be wearing a Rangers sweater throughout the arenas of Europe.

The teams started the tour with a couple of games in London in late April, then moved on to play games in Geneva and Zurich, Switzerland, Paris, France, several different cities in West Germany, and Vienna, Austria. In all, the Bruins won nine of the 23 games played, with three ending in a tie.

Though attendance in the various cities varied considerably and the tour was not a financial success, the teams put on a fine display of hockey and may have gone a long way toward creating interest in pro hockey.

FERNIE FLAMAN

When Flaman played youth hockey in Saskatchewan, it was customary for the young players to wear the numbers and names of their favorite NHL players on the backs of their sweaters. Flaman had chosen defenseman Babe Pratt as the

Fernie Flaman, the ring-leader and captain of the Bruins in the mid-to-late 1950s, was one of the most respected men on the team. An outstanding shot-blocker, he was regarded by teammates as being almost like a second goalie.

player he would honor. Fernie made his NHL debut with the Bruins in 1944 at the age of 17, but only appeared in one game. When he was called up for good from Hershey in 1947 to stay, ironically it was Pratt who was sent down to Hershey to make room for the young defenseman.

A defenseman, Flaman was called up in 1944 when one of the right wingers was injured and Art decided to press him into service on an emergency basis. Fernie wasn't expected to see much action, but before the game Ross called him aside to warn him about Bucko McDonald's devastating body checks.

The 17-year-old Flaman finally got into the game, but he forgot what Ross had told him. Trying to make a play, he had his head down and McDonald hammered him.

Flaman woke up in the dressing room but had learned a valuable lesson.

An amateur boxer of some note as a teenager back in Regina, Saskatchewan, Fernie developed a reputation as the team's "policeman" and often came to the aid of his teammates. He was paid tremendous compliments from the likes of Gordie Howe and Jean Beliveau in the mid-1950s. Howe, who was generally thought of as the toughest player in the league at that time, said it was Flaman whom he considered the toughest. Beliveau, Montreal's classy and graceful center who was also one of the larger players of his era said, "Any other player I do not worry about. But when I go near that fellow, believe me, I look over my shoulder."

Reggie Fleming

In late October of 1965, Boston papers were reporting that the Bruins were in the process of trading Fleming, sometimes called "Cement Head," to the Rangers for center Earl Ingerfeld. The deal never materialized, and it may well have been in the best interest of the Bruins in the long run. When the team finally did trade Fleming in January of 1966, they received the popular John McKenzie in return, and of course "Pie" would go on to many productive years with Boston. A week before the trade, rumors were still circulating that Fleming might be on his way to the Rangers. On January 9, while the Bruins were playing New York at Madison Square Garden, a fan hollered out during warmups, "Hey Reggie, when are you coming here?" The trade occurred the following day.

Never an overly productive offensive player in his two seasons with Boston, Reggie had what was likely his best game on October 22, 1964 at the Garden when he scored two shorthanded goals against the Maple Leafs.

John "Frosty" Forristall

The beloved trainer worked for the Bruins from 1965 through 1984. The local boy had starred as a goalie for nearby North Quincy High School before entering the marines. In the late 1960s he shared a house in Nahant, Massachusetts with Bruins Bobby Orr, Eddie Johnston, and Gary Doak. Frosty was just like one of the players, and was often involved in the shenanigans that were seemingly always occurring. During one playoff series with the Canadiens in the heyday of the "Big, Bad Bruins," "Frosty" was responsible for a minor controversy at the Montreal Forum.

When the Canadiens arrived at the Forum for practice before one of the games, they found a dummy dressed in a Canadiens uniform hanging from the balcony.

NORMAN "HEC" FOWLER

The first goalie in Bruins history, Fowler started the first seven games in the team's inaugural season of 1924-25, but his brief stay ended on a rather dubious note.

On November 22, 1924, the Bruins, with Fowler in net, lost to Toronto 10-1 at Boston Arena. The following day, Fowler admitted that after Toronto had broken a 1-1 tie, he let goals go in on purpose, figuring that if they got beat badly, coach Art Ross would go out and get better players.

Ross's first personnel move was to use a better goalie, and he immediately dumped Fowler.

ROBBIE FTOREK

As a youngster, Ftorek's family of nearby Needham, Massachussetts had season tickets to the Bruins games. When Robbie was very young, his favorite Bruins player was center Fleming MacKell. One day in the late 1950s, MacKell spotted young Robbie hanging around outside the Bruins dressing room and decided to give him a tour.

Robbie came away with a stick signed by the entire team, and a friend for life. He and MacKell kept in touch for decades after.

* * *

There was a time when the future Bruins coach incurred the wrath of the entire Boston team due to an on-ice incident while he was playing with Quebec in 1979. The Bruins played the Nordiques on November 20 of that season, and in the first period, Ftorek high-sticked Bobby Schmautz, cutting the Boston right winger's upper lip for 20 stitches and chipping three teeth. Robbie no doubt ruined Schmautz's Thanksgiving dinner, which was two days away. Ftorek may have immediately felt like a target of Bruins players, and after the game, Boston's Bobby Miller said, "That thing with Ftorek and Schmautz left a bad taste, and I don't think Ftorek wanted to play much after that." Coincidentally, the Bruins and Nordiques would be meeting again that Thanksgiving night, this time back at Boston Garden. Quebec coach Jacques Demers knew that Boston players had revenge on their minds, and brought up Paul Stewart from the minor leagues specifically to help protect Ftorek. Stewart had been born and brought up in the Boston area, and became more well known later as a referee in the NHL.

Placed on a line with Ftorek, Stewart did his job and tangled with three different Bruins in the process. Stan Jonathan took the first swipe at Robbie, punching him in the face and knocking his helmet off. Stewart fought him, as well as Terry O'Reilly and Al Secord later on before being given a

Robbie Ftorek, a Boston-area native, went from watching the Bruins from his family's season tickets to the Garden in the 1950s to standing behind the Boston bench in the early 21st century.

game misconduct very late in the third period. Meanwhile, Ftorek wasn't so intimidated that he lost his scoring touch, as he scored a goal and had two assists.

The following season, on February 8, 1981, Robbie made a nice gesture toward Stewart for the protection he provided. By that time, Paul was out of hockey, broadcasting sports for a Cape Cod station, but was at the Boston Garden that night as Quebec beat the Bruins 4-3. When Ftorek scored a goal that night, he went into the net to retrieve the puck and presented it to Stewart after the game in the Nordiques' dressing room.

Gallery Gods

This was the unique name given to the season ticket holders who occupied the first couple rows of the second balcony, high above rinkside at the old Boston Garden. Numbering as many as 1,500 at its height, the "Gods" formed a sort of a fraternity, creating their own trophy that was awarded to one Bruins player each season. They tended to embrace the tough guys and brawlers above all.

Gallinger/Taylor Betting Scandal

The incident that caused the expulsion from the NHL of Don Gallinger and Billy Taylor remains one of the darkest, most regrettable happenings in Boston Bruins history.

The wheels were set in motion for the NHL's worst scandal when Taylor was acquired by Boston from the Detroit Red Wings for Bep Guidolin on October 15, 1947. Upon his arrival, Taylor moved into the same boardinghouse in Boston's Kenmore Square where Gallinger and several other Bruins were staying. Taylor, a 28-year-old center was a fine stickhandler and playmaker, and some on the Bruins felt he had the chance to be one of the best who ever played the game. He was even thought by some to be "the next Bill Cowley." But Taylor also had a reputation throughout the league as a gambler, and there were even rumors that he had bet on Maple Leafs games while he was playing for them. Taylor had heard similar types of rumors about Gallinger, who had joined the Bruins as a 17-year-old in the 1942-43 season.

During a card game at the boardinghouse between the two that fall, Taylor asked Gallinger if he was interested in making some easy money. Taylor explained to his teammate that he could double his $7,500-per-year salary by betting on his team to lose, if he carefully selected the right games. He specified that if the Bruins were on the road against a tough opponent, and possibly if there were key players injured or not playing up to par, even with everyone's best effort, they would be likely to lose. Taylor's philosophy seemed to be that if the outcome was virtually inevitable, why not make money on the outcome? Taylor also told Gallinger that he knew a bookie in Detroit who would handle the action. On a subsequent road trip, he introduced him to the man, a career criminal named James Tamer who was well known to the Detroit police.

In the minds of Taylor and Gallinger, they weren't throwing games intentionally, they were simply taking advantage of games in which the odds were strongly against the Bruins winning.

By late January of that season, Taylor not only had played well below expectations, but Bruins management was very suspicious of his activities. The team felt it was time to dispose of a potential problem and sent Taylor home to Oshawa, with team president Weston Adams announcing that he would play no more for Boston. Taylor was finally traded to the Rangers on February 6, 1948.

On February 17, the Bruins arrived in Chicago for a game against the Blackhawks the following evening. Gallinger knew that the Bruins would have their hands full as star center Milt

Schmidt was back home with a knee injury and defensman Clare Martin was also out. He placed a call to Tamer to bet $1,500 on Chicago to win. Tamer immediately contacted Taylor in New York, who put $500 down on the Bruins to lose. What none of the men were aware of was that the Detroit police were monitoring Tamer very closely and had placed a wiretap on his phone.

A week later, after the Bruins had actually won the game in question against Chicago 4-2, the news broke that Detroit police had uncovered a betting scandal involving two unnamed NHL players. In reviewing the wiretap, they came across Gallinger's conversation with Tamer and Tamer's phone call to Taylor immediately after. The league was notified, and president Clarence Campbell began an investigation.

Bruins coach Art Ross and owner Adams questioned every player on the team, but Gallinger would admit nothing. Most of the players, however, strongly suspected that he was involved. Campbell came to Boston the following week with the transcripts of the wiretap and told Gallinger that he would be suspended indefinitely for associating with a known gambler. The next day, Ross received a call from Detroit informing him that Gallinger owed money for a gambling debt, and the coach's worst fears were confirmed. It was said after that Ross was devastated by the scandal, and he was heartbroken that a Bruins player would become involved.

Campbell then announced that both Gallinger and Taylor would be banned from the NHL permanently. Eventually, Gallinger confessed all of the details to Campbell, but the president would not show leniency. Decades later, Gallinger said that he had bet on the Bruins to win several times per season since his rookie year of 1942-43, but he had never bet on them to lose until he hooked up with Taylor in 1947. Gallinger claimed to have bet against Boston about a half dozen times that season.

Finally in 1970, 22 years after the scandal, the two banned players were reinstated by Campbell. Taylor later went to work as a scout for the Washington Capitals, while Gallinger never worked in the league again.

BERT GARDINER

The journeyman goaltender was wrapping up his career with the Bruins during the 1943-44 season, and had become the starting goalie largely because Frankie Brimsek and several other competent goalies were serving in the military in World War II. Gardiner made quite an impression on November 21, 1943 when he allowed 13 goals in a 13-4 loss to the Canadiens in Montreal. Bert was remembered by his teammates as a man who had a fondness for alcohol, and a week after the Montreal debacle as the team was set to embark on a train trip to Toronto, coach Art Ross detected Gardiner had been drinking and wouldn't allow him on the train. Bert did end up playing in 41 of the team's 50 games that season, but ended with a woeful 5.17 goals-against average. He would never cast his shadow over an NHL crease again.

By the time the Bruins arrived in Toronto for their game against the Maple Leafs, minus Bert Gardiner, Coach Ross had realized that he had no spare goaltender. After consulting with hockey associates in Toronto, it appeared that Ross's best option was the Maple Leafs practice goalie named George Abbott, who happened to be a 47-year-old minister who had never played one minute of professional hockey. When Abbott arrived at the Bruins' dressing room before the game, the team trainer took one look, thought it was a joke, and wouldn't let him in.

After being convinced that this was indeed the Bruins goalie for the evening, Abbott was allowed to enter, but as he was dressing for the game he was so nervous he started to put his skates on the wrong feet. After straightening that out, he went to go out on the ice and opened a door that led him, in full uniform, out into the crowded lobby of Maple Leaf Gardens.

Remarkably, Abbott only allowed seven goals in the 7-4 Bruins loss, and it is not surprising that George would not get a second chance to put his skates on correctly on the first try again.

JEAN-GUY GENDRON

The left wing from Montreal, Quebec served two tours of duty with the Bruins, but was involved in a noteworthy incident while with the New York Rangers during the 1961-62 season. Gendron engaged in a vicious stick fight with Bruins rookie defenseman Ted Green, for which both players were fined $200 by the league.

After that season, Gendron was claimed by Boston in the intra-league draft. He was given the stall right next to Green in the Bruins' dressing room that fall, and surprisingly, the two became very close friends.

Hal Gill

At 6'7," 240 pounds, Gill entered 2003 as the largest to ever don the Bruins sweater. He was born in Concord, Massachussetts, not far from Boston, and growing up a Bruins fan, he idolized Ray Bourque as a youngster. Wanting to be just like Bourque, he always made sure he wore No. 7 in youth hockey and played defense.

He couldn't believe it when he finally got the chance to play alongside his hero in 1997.

Gold Pants of 1959

Early in 1959 the Bruins may have been guilty of sporting the most hideous uniform combination in their long history. To go along with their attractive gold jerseys, the team abandoned its traditional black hockey pants in favor of matching gold. The new look was universally unpopular with the players and gave them a garish look vaguely similar to the Los Angeles Kings' yellow-gold uniform a decade later.

Another aspect of the bright gold pants that troubled the players was the fact that when they got stains on the backside from sliding on and off the dirty bench, it invited off-color and uncomplimentary comments from fans and opposing players.

Management had the good sense to discontinue the gold pants after a couple dozen games.

TED GREEN

In the mid-1960s, prior to the arrival of Orr and Esposito, "Terrible" Ted was one of the heroes of faithful Bruins fans. He was one of the toughest and meanest Bruins ever, and was regarded by some as the "new Eddie Shore" in terms of his demeanor on the ice.

Green was involved in one of the scariest near-tragedies in Bruins history when St. Louis Blues forward Wayne Maki hit him in the head with the heel of the blade of his stick in an exhibition game in Ottawa on September 21, 1969. Green suffered a severely fractured skull, and his comeback a year later was nothing short of miraculous. Ted himself admitted much later that he had tempted fate by even appearing in the preseason game in which he was struck by Maki. The Bruin defenseman had just agreed verbally to a new contract but had not yet signed it and actually considered sitting out until the formality had occurred.

One odd coincidence of the unfortunate incident was that Green had been a defensive partner of former Bruin Tom Johnson (later a Bruins coach and front-office executive) at the time Johnson's career was abruptly ended when Chico Maki, Wayne's brother, had skated over the back of his leg in 1965.

After Green came home from his extended stay in the hospital, he made up his mind that he was going to attempt a rehabilitation to see if he could make it back to the Bruins. In the summer of 1970, he worked out in Lynnfield, Massachussetts, with trainer Gene Berde, who was credited with totally reworking the physique of Boston Red Sox outfielder Carl Yastrzemski a few years earlier. Green had to work tremendously hard to fully regain the use of his extremities, particularly his left hand, as he was left-handed.

When Green reported to Bruins training camp in London, Ontario, in September of 1970, all of his teammates wondered if he would be able to skate well enough. It appeared that his skating was unaffected by the injury and the long layoff, and everyone was so moved and encouraged that they began to believe that he would make it back. Still, the going was very rough at times, and his confidence was shaken on occasion when he felt he couldn't perform exactly as he had before. On December 2, 1970 in Chicago he got into his first fight since his return, beating Don Maloney. This turned out to be a tremendous boost to his confidence, making him believe he had really turned the corner.

On January 24, 1971, Green was the recipient of a showering of affection on "Ted Green Night" at the Boston Garden. Interestingly enough, plans for such a tribute had first been discussed several months before the injury that caused him to miss a year, but his valiant comeback made it even more meaningful.

In the pregame ceremony, Green was extremely emotional, nearly breaking down several times. Among the gifts he was presented with were a new red station wagon, a snow blower, a stereo system, a freezer, and from Bruins management, blueprints to an addition for his house as well as a check to pay for it. Green then went out and played one of the finest, most inspired games since his comeback as the Bruins beat Montreal 4-2.

*   *   *

In the late 1960s, Ted's teammates would tease him because they thought he looked Jewish, and took to calling him "Abie." One time in the locker room he told general manager Milt Schmidt that he couldn't play that day. When Schmidt asked why, Green replied that it was a Jewish holiday, which broke up the entire room.

BEP GUIDOLIN

The Bruins' coach from 1972 to 1974 acquired the nickname "Bep," which is the Italian equivalent of "baby" at a very young age from his parents and two older sisters. Discovered playing junior hockey with his local area Oshawa Generals, Guidolin was able to rise to the NHL level before the age of 17 due to rosters being depleted from players entering the service during World War II. The Bruins had lost the services of their famed "Kraut Line"—Milt Schmidt, Woody Dumart, and Bobby Bauer, Roy Conacher, and others. Guidolin was signed by Boston in early November of 1942, and joined them in Toronto on November 12 to make his NHL debut. He was placed on the so-called "Sprout Line," a takeoff on the Kraut Line, named because all three members of the line were still in their teens. One of Bep's linemates was the ill-fated Don Gallinger, destined to be banned from the game for betting.

Unfortunately, because of wartime restrictions, Guidolin had visa problems and was unable to leave Ontario to travel with the Bruins for nearly two weeks. He did not play with the team again until November 24 against Chicago in Boston, and managed to score his first NHL goal in the 5-5 tie. He

The future Bruins coach was pictured here as a teenage player with Boston in the early 1940s.

went on to see regular ice time and was making a positive impression in the process.

To this day, Guidolin holds the distinction of being the youngest player to ever appear in an NHL game, making his debut at 16 years, 11 months, and three days old. But a seemingly forgotten claim from Bep himself less than a month into his rookie season may cast doubt on the distinction entirely. On the occasion of what was thought to be his 17th birthday, December 9, Guidolin told a Boston reporter that there was a mix-up on his reported birth date and that he was really turning 18 that day.

If Bep was correct about the year of his birth, there would in reality be several players who began their NHL careers at an earlier age than him.

CHRIS HAYES

For left wing Hayes, his extremely brief Bruins career was a matter of right place, right time. The former teammate of Bobby Orr with the Oshawa Generals for two seasons in the mid-1960s was called up for the playoffs in 1972. He was given a couple of shifts during one of the games, and as a result, his name is forever engraved on Lord Stanley's Cup.

JOHN HENDERSON

On January 12, 1956, Bruins starting goalie Terry Sawchuk broke the little finger on his right hand in warmups before a game versus Chicago, although he managed to play through the entire game in obvious pain. In need of a replacement, Boston remembered the good job young John Henderson had done in a backup role the previous season, and called him up from Hershey to start the next game in Montreal.

Unfortunately, when Henderson arrived from Hershey on the day of the game, his equipment did not arrive with him. Finding another set of equipment was complicated by the fact that "Long" John wore size 13 skates and a pair that large could not be found. This paved the way for the NHL debut of the Canadiens practice goalie Claude Pronovost, who was pressed into service on an emergency basis.

Pronovost did quite well for himself and his temporary team as he shut out Montreal 2-0 to snap an 11-game Bruins winless streak. While he would never don the Boston sweater again, Pronovost did get the chance to appear in two Canadiens games three seasons later.

As for Henderson, his skates finally arrived and he was able to play the following game, losing 4-1 to Toronto in Boston. Though he was still playing pro hockey 13 years later, he never again appeared in an NHL game. In December of 1967 when a much younger Andre Gill was called up to Boston for a brief trial, it was Henderson who was serving as his backup down in Hershey.

JIM HENRY

"Sugar Jim" as he was known came to the Bruins before the 1951-52 season, and played every minute of every game in goal for Boston for the next three seasons. In Game 6 of the 1952 playoffs against Montreal he took a Doug Harvey shot between the eyes. His eyes became blackened and swollen almost shut, and as difficult as it is to imagine today, he went out and played Game 7 two days later.

JIMMY HERBERT

The Bruins' original number No. 4, Herbert was the team's first true star player, emerging as a scoring force in their inaugural season of 1924-25. It was that season that he would be the only player in team history to lead the Bruins in goals, assists, points, and penalty minutes in the same season.

By 1927, Art Ross felt that Herbert's skills had declined. When Toronto's coach, Conn Smythe, was looking for talent, Ross recommended Herbert and ultimately sold him to the Leafs for $15,000.

It didn't take Smythe long to realize he had been taken, and what would be a long bitter feud with Ross was underway. Smythe disposed of the disappointing Herbert to Detroit less than four months later.

LIONEL HITCHMAN

The Bruins defenseman for whom uniform No. 3 is retired was acquired by Art Ross from Ottawa midway through Boston's first season. He served as the Bruins' first team captain and later was a defensive partner of Eddie Shore for many seasons. In December of 1925, sportswriter Fred Moey referred to him as "tall, fearless, and reckless," and called him the most daring hockey player ever seen in this city. It must be remembered that Eddie Shore did not come to the Bruins until the following season, but Hitchman appeared to have something else in common with Shore that does not appear to be commonly remembered. When Moey added, referring to Lionel, "so when Boston hockey fans watch No. 2 of the Boston Bruins...." he seemed to be revealing a little-known fact that Hitchman wore Shore's No. 2 on his Boston jersey before Shore did, and before Lionel's much more well-known No. 3. When Hitchman retired in February of 1934, the Bruins were said to have retired his No. 3, although they allowed "Flash" Hollet to wear it for a while later on before putting it away for good.

Hitchman had served as a Royal Canadian Mountie before entering the NHL, but left them in 1921. It was said that braving the snow on horseback in the hinterlands of the frozen north, subsisting on a diet of icicle pops and snowball sundaes wasn't for him. He found it rather dull, and wanting more action, he found it in the NHL.

Hitchman and Sprague Cleghorne were bitter enemies when Lionel was with Ottawa and Sprague was with the Canadiens, and Hitch even needed a trip to the hospital when Cleghorne hit him in the head with a stick. When Cleghorne was traded to the Bruins in November of 1925 he entered the Boston dressing room where Art Ross introduced the two, even though they were well known to each other. Hitchman stuck out his hand and said, "If we can team up on defense with as much vigor and energy as we did against each other, we should keep the league away from our net."

KEN HODGE JR.

Ken recalls, "My father wanted me to play baseball instead of hockey. With a name that was already known in hockey, he thought there would be too much pressure on me."

Young Hodge still forged ahead and pursued a career in hockey, playing for Boston College for three seasons, and later making his NHL debut with Minnesota in 1989. In August of 1990 he was acquired by Boston for a draft choice, and the son of No. 8 for the Bruins would play on a line with another No. 8 (Cam Neely).

On February 5, 1991, Hodge scored a hat trick that included the winning goal in overtime in a 6-5 win over Edmonton. That spring he won channel 38's "Seventh Player Award." In June of that season he was named to the NHL "All-Rookie" team, just as his brother Dan, a defenseman at Merrimack College was being drafted in the ninth round of the amateur draft by the Bruins.

"Flash" Hollett

The defenseman came to the Bruins in 1936 when he was sold by the Toronto Maple Leafs for a mere $16,000. Shortly after, both Eddie Shore and Dit Clapper encouraged him to rush the puck more often because of his considerable stickhandling skills. Three years later he had the chance to gain revenge on Toronto for dumping him as he scored the goal against them to win the 1939 Stanley Cup finals.

In his time with the Bruins, Hollett had the distinction of wearing both Shore's No. 2 and Lionel Hitchman's No. 3.

Bronco Horvath

The center on the popular "Uke Line" with Johnny Bucyk and Vic Stasiuk, it was Bucyk who stated that Horvath, whose real first name was Bronco, had the most accurate wrist shot he ever saw. He put it to good use on February 8, 1959 as he scored three goals, two of which were shorthanded in a 4-1 win over the New York Rangers at the Boston Garden.

He had managed to attract attention that game for more than having to wear a face mask to protect his broken jaw.

*   *   *

As the 1959-60 season was winding down, Horvath was in a very close race with young Blackhawks left wing Bobby Hull for the NHL scoring title. Heading into the final game of the regular season, Chicago was in Boston to play the Bruins, who had been recently eliminated from playoff contention. Horvath, with 80 points at that point, held a one-point lead over Hull, and with little else to cheer for, Bruins fans were shouting relentlessly for Bronco to capture the title.

In the first period, Horvath was struck in the jaw with a slapshot off the stick of teammate Bob Armstrong, and had to be taken to nearby Massachusetts General Hospital. In the meantime, much to the dismay of the Garden crowd, Hull scored a goal and assisted on another goal to win the title by one mere point. The assist was rather fluky when a pass bounced off a teammate's skate and went into the Bruins net.

AL IAFRATE

The burly defenseman who had earned the nickname "Wild Thing" was scheduled to report to Bruins training camp in September of 1995. Players were expected at the training site in Wilmington, Massachussetts, on 9:00 that first morning, but big Al was nowhere to be found.

Finally, around 12:30 that afternoon, Iafrate cruised into the parking lot on his Harley-Davidson motorcycle. As he was getting off the bike, Bruins vice president Tom Johnson happened to be walking out of the building. Without even looking up or stopping as he passed Iafrate, Johnson said calmly, "That'll cost you $500, Al."

Iafrate got right back on his motorcycle and rode away. As it turned out, he never played another game for the Bruins.

EDDIE JOHNSTON

Eddie made his NHL debut with the Bruins on December 15, 1962, and went on to play in the next 160 straight games. In the 1963-64 season, Johnston was to be the last NHL goalie to play all of his team's games in a season, logging every minute of the 70-game schedule. In a time when Johnston, like most NHL goalies did not wear a mask, he broke his nose three times in a week and a half, yet still missed no time.

Breaking his nose three times would have been preferable to what Johnston went through in the fall of 1968. The veteran goaltender had gotten off to a great start that season, but Halloween night in Detroit would change everything. In warmups before that night's game with the Red Wings, a slapshot off the stick of Bobby Orr fractured his skull and very nearly killed him. Normally there would only be one puck used for practice shots, but this night there happened to be two. Both Orr and Eddie Shack were ready to shoot, and Johnston thought Shack would go first, but the shot came from Orr's direction and Johnston never saw it. For the next six or seven weeks, Eddie barely knew what was going on. At least twice during that time, he was given his last rites by a priest.

In and out of a coma, Johnston experienced severe swelling of the brain and lost a total of 40 pounds during that time. Finally, just before Christmas of 1968, he began to improve and was able to get back between the pipes early in 1969. Eddie went on to be a key member of the Stanley Cup winning teams of 1970 and 1972.

STAN JONATHAN

The member of the Tuscarora Indian Tribe was a noted pugilist and favorite of the Gallery Gods. Don Cherry claimed that Stan really enjoyed fighting, and that he even studied his on-ice fights blow by blow on videotape.

One of his more noteworthy and popular decisions came against Montreal's Pierre Bouchard in the 1978 Stanley Cup Finals. Bouchard, who was six inches taller and 30 pounds heavier, was pummeled senseless by Jonathan.

* * *

Don Cherry sent Jonathan down to the minors during the 1977-78 season after he had scored eight goals in a ten-game span. Cherry admitted that he did so to get Stan back to his game, which was primarily to be physiCalifornia The coach knew that when a player who wasn't a scorer started to score a lot, he would start to think he was Gordie Howe, and would get away from the style that got him to the NHL in the first place.

In January of 1980 when Cherry came to Boston as the new coach of the Colorado Rockies, Jonathan scored his only career hat trick to help the Bruins beat the Rockies 6-2. Jonathan had always been a favorite of Cherry, and all Grapes could say after the game was, "If anybody had to get three goals against us, I'm glad it was Stanley."

JOE JUNKIN

Countless boys who grew up in Canada in the 1950s dreamed of a career in the NHL, but likely none envisioned a career that lasted a grand total of eight minutes.

Goalie Joe Junkin can in retrospect say that he had a career in the NHL, and that he retired with a goals-against average of 0.00, but it all requires a bit of explanation.

When Eddie Johnston suffered a fractured skull in late October of 1968, Junkin was one of the minor leaguers called up, coming from Oklahoma City to serve as Gerry Cheevers's backup. Joe finally got the chance to take the ice as Cheevers's replacement for the final eight minutes of Boston's wild 10-5 win over Chicago on December 14, 1968. Among the more noteworthy occurrences in the game was Phil Esposito's hat trick.

As for Junkin, it was back to the minor leagues shortly after, with his NHL career now concluded.

DOUG KEANS

Goalie Keans may well have represented the best $100 the Bruins have spent in many a decade. Picked up from the Los Angeles Kings in May of 1983 for that modest sum, the 5'7" goalie gave them an unexpectedly good season in 1984-85.

On January 16, 1984 he recorded his first NHL shutout, and went on to a 19-8-3 record with a team-leading 3.10 goals-against average.

GORD KLUZAK

Gord was selected first overall in the 1982 amateur draft despite the opinion of some that Brian Bellows should have been selected instead. Fate was not kind to Kluzak and the Bruins, and after 11 knee surgeries he was forced to retire in 1991 at the age of 27. Gordie, who claimed to have babysat for NHL center Shaun Van Allen as a child enrolled in Harvard University. He graduated with a degree in economics in 1994, and went on to Harvard Business school, where he graduated in 1998.

BILLY KNIBBS

It has been written and long believed that the hockey career of Bruins rookie center Billy Knibbs was essentially ended in January of 1965 when he was viciously checked by Red Wings legend Gordie Howe. Though there is little question that Howe's check of Knibbs was outside the parameters of good, clean hockey, it did not affect Billy's ability to play professionally, which he did for 10 more years.

During that game at the Garden, Knibbs had stolen the puck away from Howe in front of the Bruins net, and Howe went on to chase him down and check him very hard from behind into the boards near the Bruins bench. Knibbs was later taken to a nearby hospital for observation, but was able to resume playing within a few days. Billy went on to play nearly the rest of the season for Boston. Come the NHL waiver draft that June, the New York Rangers selected Knibbs off the Bruins roster because they had observed that he had played well against them that season and felt he had potential. He was ultimately never able to crack the Rangers' lineup, but played at the top level of minor-league hockey until 1975.

The "Kraut Line"

From their early teenage years in Kitchener, Ontario, Milt Schmidt, Woody Dumart, and Bobby Bauer seemed destined to make names for themselves individually and collectively on the ice. By the time they were all between the ages of 19 and 21, the three childhood friends were teamed up on a Bruins line that was originally called the "Sauerkraut Line" because of their German heritage. It was shortened to "Kraut Line," and when World War II broke out, they were more commonly referred to as the "Kitchener Kids" due to the prevailing anti-German sentiment.

The three linemates were so close that they enlisted in the Royal Canadian Air Force together in 1942. In one of the

The legendary Bruins trio of (left to right) Bobby Bauer, Milt Schmidt, and Woody Dumart.

most emotional scenes to have occurred at the Boston Garden to that point, a celebration was held after their final game. In that game on February 10, 1942 versus Montreal in which Boston won 8-1, the Kraut Line accounted for eight points. In a tearful farewell, the three men were carried off the ice by members of *both* teams. The line returned safely from the war and was reunited in the fall of 1945.

The lack of ego between the three childhood friends was such that they all agreed that they should be paid the same.

Orland Kurtenbach

The tough journeyman center got on the wrong side of the Gallery Gods early in the 1964-65 season when, after getting off to a very slow start stated that he had trouble getting going before Christmas.

The next game at the Garden, the Gods showed up wearing Santa Claus hats and singing Christmas carols every time Kurtenbach touched the puck.

Gus Kyle

The big defenseman from Saskatchewan had his last go-round in the NHL with Boston in the 1951-52 season. Like Bruins great defenseman Lionel Hitchman, Kyle had served time in the Royal Canadian Mounted Police. The Mounties had a rule forbidding marriage until a patrolman had served seven years. Kyle met the woman he wanted to marry well before the seven-year mark, and managed to buy his way out of the force, paving the way for both his marriage and his NHL career.

Leo Labine

Leo was an intensely scrappy right winger who was a fan favorite on the Bruins team throughout the 1950s. His lack of fear was evident in a game against Montreal when he had a run-in with rugged Canadiens defenseman Butch Bouchard, who was four inches taller and 40 pounds heavier. As the two

Right winger Leo Labine in the early 1950s.

came nose to nose, Labine indignantly spewed out, "You've got 32 teeth, Butch. Would you like to try for 16?" All Butch could do at that point was laugh so hard he nearly doubled over.

In the mid-1950s as the Bruins were traveling by train to Toronto, they pulled into a station for a stop along the way. The players would often take advantage of these stops to get off to grab a bite to eat or just stretch their legs. Labine and teammate Real Chevrefils got off wearing only their pajamas and slippers, but when it was time to get back on board, they got on the wrong train. As the train was pulling away, they spotted their teammates on the other train laughing.

Luckily, the two pajama-clad hockey players were able to rejoin their pals as both trains made a stop much later at the same station.

AL "JUNIOR" LANGLOIS

The defenseman had a nine-year career in the NHL that concluded with the Bruins after the 1965-66 season. He has the distinction of being the last player to wear No. 4 for the Bruins before the great Bobby Orr.

GUY LAPOINTE

The veteran defenseman was one of the favorites of Montreal youth Ray Bourque, who was no doubt pleased when Lapointe scored a goal in the famous "too many men on the ice game" in the 1979 playoffs. Bourque would not be drafted by Boston until one month later. Lapointe, incidentally, was taken off the ice on a stretcher late in the third period of that noteworthy Bruins-Canadiens game, and was not available when Yvon Lambert scored the winning goal in overtime.

Bourque would be thrilled four years later when Lapointe joined him on the Bruins' defensive corps. Guy had learned some of the finer points of defensive play from such greats as J.C. Tremblay and Jacques Laperriere, and would pass his knowledge on to Bourque and Gord Kluzak, with whom he was often paired.

Lapointe had arrived with the Bruins just as Brad Park was departing. Park had just informed the team that he was signing with Detroit when Lapointe signed with Boston on Aug. 15, 1983. When Harry Sinden was asked how long it took him to go after Guy, who had played the previous two seasons with St. Louis, he said as soon as Park walked out of his office.

But shortly after the 1983-84 season began, a minor controversy erupted involving Lapointe. The Bruins allowed him to wear No. 5, which had been his number throughout his career, but had been retired by Boston in honor of the great Dit Clapper back in 1947. Many were not pleased with the decision, including Clapper's family. After 19 games, the Bruins announced on November 22, 1983 that "by mutual consent" Lapointe would switch to No. 27 and that Clapper's sacred No. 5 would be once again taken out of circulation.

THE "LAST HURRAH"

On September 26, 1995, the Bruins celebrated the closing of the old Boston Garden with an exhibition game versus their longtime rivals, the Montreal Canadiens. As part of the festivities, many beloved former Bruins were on hand to give the ancient arena a proper sendoff. Legendary Bruins Bobby Orr, Phil Esposito, John Bucyk, and Milt Schmidt were there to personally lower their retired number banners from the rafters for the trip to the new Fleet Center.

Not surprisingly, Orr received the loudest ovation of the evening, but the most heartwarming, even tear-jerking moment involved former left wing Normand Leveille, who had been felled by a cerebral hemorrhage 13 years earlier. To the surprise of all, Normand appeared on skates, and when announced, was helped out on the ice by Raymond Bourque. Later on, the former Bruins had the opportunity to skate a few final laps around the Garden ice, and Normand was assisted around the rink by Terry O' Reilly on one side, Bourque on the other. As singer Rene Rancourt sang "Auld Lang Syne," tears were flowing freely throughout the venerable old building.

When the ceremonies had concluded and nearly everyone had left, it was Orr who fittingly took the final skate around the old Garden ice, 25 years after he soared through the air, just having scored the Stanley Cup-winning goal.

*   *   *

Local fan Fred Bramante had lived five minutes away from the Boston Garden back in 1928, and was an avid follower of sporting events. He was in attendance for the first event ever held there, a night of professional boxing on November 17, and came back three days later for the Bruins' first game. Bramante, living just over the New Hampshire border in Salem in 1995 was also on hand to help say goodbye to the old barn as he was there for the "Last Hurrah."

*   *   *

On a humorous note, "The Last Hurrah" evening also featured Terry O'Reilly, Fernie Flaman, and Stan Jonathan having their picture taken together in the penalty box—a place where all three felt very much at home.

JEFF LAZARO

The left wing from Waltham, Massachusetts who played with Boston from 1990 to '92 drew a great deal of inspiration as an athlete from his courageous uncle Joe Lazaro. A Waltham native also, Joe lost his sight in World War II, but began golfing six years later, in 1950. He went on to become the National Blind Golfers' Champion seven times.

Shortly after Jeff had realized his dream of playing for the Bruins, he recalled of his uncle, "He always told me to 'keep working hard, you'll get noticed.'"

STEVE LEACH

When Steve was a young hockey fan of 6 years old growing up near Boston, he could not be blamed for being interested in knowing that a player by the name of Reggie Leach was a right wing for his favorite team. Twenty years later when fate intervened and brought Steve to the Bruins, the new right winger was given the same No. 27 worn by Reggie in his Boston days.

Richie Leduc

Leduc was playing for the Bruins' top farm team, the Boston Braves in January of 1973, and was meeting his fiancee and her parents to watch the Bruins play at the Garden on the night of January 11. He had just parked his car in the Garden parking lot when Sinden waved to him. Thinking Sinden was just saying "hi," he waved back. The general manager then rushed over and told Leduc he was being promoted to the Bruins due to an injury to Gregg Sheppard.

Richie's fiancee got an unexpected surprise, as she got to witness him making his NHL debut that night.

Normand Leveille

The story of Normand is truly one of the saddest in all of Boston Bruins history. In June of 1981, the French speaking left wing had become the youngest player ever drafted by the Bruins, taken with the 14th overall pick in the first round. Leveille made the team in his first training camp and had a very promising rookie season in 1981-82. Knowing barely a word of English when he came to the team, he relied heavily on Bruins assistant coach Jean Ratelle as an interpreter.

Considered one of the NHL's rising young stars, Normand got off to fine start in the fall of 1982. On October 14, in a game against Vancouver at Boston Garden, he scored the only two Boston goals in a 2-1 Bruins win. Nine days later on October 23, the Bruins traveled to Vancouver to meet the Canucks again, with Leveille as the team's leading scorer. In the first period, he was checked very hard by Vancouver's Marc Crawford, yet was able to take a couple more shifts before the end of the period. Before the start of the second period he complained of dizziness, then passed out in the Bruins' dressing room. He was rushed to Vancouver General Hospital where a CAT scan revealed a congenital condition described by doctors as an arteriovenous malformation. They made it clear that it was very unlikely that it would have been caused by being checked, and that it could have even been triggered by just a sneeze.

That night, Leveille underwent six hours of surgery, during which it was discovered that significant damage had been done to his brain. His life hung in the balance for days, and while he would survive, he was left permanently disabled at the age of 19.

Two years later, Normand returned to the Boston Garden for the first time to a heartwarming welcome. On November 11, 1984 he came back to watch his former team play the Edmonton Oilers. In a special pregame ceremony, Normand was escorted out on the ice wearing his number 19 Bruins jersey and was introduced to the crowd. The 14,451 in attendance gave him a two-minute standing ovation in an extremely emotional scene.

CRAIG MACTAVISH

A center for the Bruins from 1979 through 1984, Mac-Tavish is often remembered as the last NHL player to play without a helmet, but he may have also been the last player to hitchhike to a game in which he played.

Though Craig had made his Boston debut on December 23, 1979, the night several Bruins jumped into the Madison Square Garden stands to defend themselves, he was playing for Springfield of the AHL a year later. On December 17, 1980, he was called back up to the Bruins and was told to report to Hartford for a game that night against the Whalers. On his way to the Hartford Civic Center, his car broke down on Route 291 about 20 miles away from the arena.

So there he stood out on the expressway with a large bag of equipment and several hockey sticks with his thumb out. After about 15 minutes he was picked up by a motorist who was heading to New York. He paid the man to drive him all the way to the Civic Center where he saw action that night.

SILVIO MANTHA

The Hall of Fame defenseman came to Boston to play his final season with the Bruins in the 1936-37 season. When he skated out on the Garden ice for the first time in a Bruins sweater in the fall of 1936, many no doubt remembered that he had scored the first goal in the history of the Boston Garden eight years prior as a member of the Montreal Canadiens, November 20, 1928.

Johnny McKenzie

After the Bruins had won the Stanley Cup in May of 1970 for the first time in 29 years, an enormous celebration was held in Boston two days later. The players were paraded through the streets and were brought to City Hall Plaza where many of them gave speeches to an adoring public. One highlight came during Boston mayor Kevin White's address to the crowd as the impish McKenzie snuck up and poured a pitcher of beer all over him.

Two years later after the Bruins won their next Stanley Cup, the Bruins were invited to Mayor White's office as part of the celebration. At one point the Mayor said he wanted to present a special award to McKenzie for his "spirit, enthusiasm, and energy," and proceeded to dump a pitcher of beer over an unsuspecting Johnny's head as everyone in the room howled with laughter. Said a soaked McKenzie, "He waited two years, but he got even!"

*   *   *

McKenzie was traded to the Bruins on January 10, 1966 from the Rangers, and there was some awkwardness when he first walked into the Bruins' dressing room. Two weeks before on Christmas night in a game against the Bruins at Boston, Johnny had elbowed Teddy Green, which touched off a melee the next night when the teams met in New York, The two became friendly in time and were able to put the incident behind them.

In McKenzie's first game with the Bruins, which was against Chicago on January 13, 1966, he was put on a line with Tommy Williams and Johnny Bucyk. Though it wouldn't mean much at the time, it is interesting to note that Phil Esposito scored a goal for the Blackhawks in the game.

PETER MCNAB

Peter's father, Max, was a center for Detroit in the late 1940s and early '50s, and by the 1960s was running the San Diego Gulls of the Western Hockey League. As a result, Peter spent several of his formative hockey playing years in San Diego, and playing a lot of his youth hockey in the Los Angeles area. Because his father had constant access to the ice rink in San Diego, Peter often had the chance to spend many hours alone practicing there, where he developed, in particular, his terrific wrist shot.

* * *

After retirement as an active player, McNab became a color commentator for the Colorado Avalanche and got to see the end of the career of his former teammate Ray Bourque up close. Having scored 363 NHL goals of his own, McNab had no reason to be starstruck, yet he recognized the greatness and uniqueness of Bourque and decided that he wanted a keepsake from the defenseman.

Peter remembered that each day after the team's morning skate, Bourque would take the laces out of his skates, throw them in the trash, and replace them with new laces. On the morning of the second game of the 2001 Stanley Cup Finals McNab hung around the Rockies' dressing room until everyone left, then reached into the trash barrel and retrieved Bourque's laces to keep as a souvenir. He then brought them home and put them in his own skates, where they remain to this day.

RICK MIDDLETON

From very early in his career, Middleton was considered one of the very best one-on-one players in the NHL. Brad Park recalls, "When he first came up to the Rangers, I had been in the league six or seven years, and he had moves I'd never seen." But when he played for New York for two seasons in his early twenties, he was thought by some to have a bit of a discipline problem and was embracing life in New York City. After Phil Esposito's first season with the Rangers, he realized that he missed his linemate Ken Hodge and asked Rangers G.M. John Ferguson to acquire him from Boston. When Ferguson and Harry Sinden began discussing a possible trade, Sinden first requested left wing Steve Vickers in exchange for Hodge, but Ferguson refused. They finally agreed on Middleton for Hodge, and the deal was completed on May 26, 1976. Bruins coach Don Cherry helped to put Rick on the right path and even received a letter from Middleton's parents thanking him for the effect he had on their son.

As time went by, Sinden once again looked like a genius. Hodge went on to play a season and a half for New York, while Middleton, nine and a half years younger than Hodge, went on to score 402 goals for Boston.

"Nifty" was known to engage in the rather unathletic practice of smoking cigarettes in between periods of hockey games in order to relax. One teammate remembered that as the season wore on, Middleton's mouth guard would become increasingly yellow. "I was afraid it was going to get up and walk away on its own!" the teammate joked.

MIKE MILBURY

Born in Boston's Brighton section and raised in Walpole, Massachusetts, Mike Milbury served his boyhood team in a variety of capacities in his decade-and-a-half affiliation with them. Aside from serving as a Bruins defensman for 11 seasons, he acted as the coach of their AHL farm team, the Maine Mariners; served as a co-coach of the Bruins with Terry O'Reilly briefly; was an assistant coach; the team's head coach from 1989 to 1991, and finally was the assistant general manager under Harry Sinden.

Regarded as an extremely articulate and analytical individual, one of Milbury's most memorable acts was beating an opposing fan with his own shoe during a major donnybrook. The date was December 23, 1979, and the place was the unfriendly confines of New York's Madison Square Garden.

An argument began on the ice between Rangers goalie John Davidson and Bruins left wing Al Secord when a fan began throwing food at Bruins players. Another fan reached over the glass to the Bruins bench and punched Stan Jonathan, cutting his nose and then stealing his stick. At this time a handful of

Bruins players jumped into the stands, including Jonathan, Terry O'Reilly, Peter McNab, and Milbury. As goalie Jim Craig would say a couple of years later, "The Bruins have become like an Irish family. Hit one brother and you've got four more to battle." O'Reilly had one of the unruly fans in a headlock, and in between glancing blows off his skull asked him, "Are you getting your money's worth?" Milbury at this time had grabbed the shoe off the foot of one of the unruly fans who was kicking at him and began pummeling him with it, creating one of the more noteworthy highlights in Bruins history.

Ranger fans had become ornery over the fact that the Rangers had been leading 3-1 going into the third period, but allowed Boston to score three unanswered goals to take a 4-3 lead. The tying goal had come when coach Don Cherry had pulled goalie Cheevers in favor of a sixth skater, and the go-ahead fourth goal soon followed. With five seconds remaining, Esposito had a breakaway and was stopped by Cheevers.

Four New York fans were arrested and charged with disorderly conduct during the melee, and with many other gathering near the Bruins team bus, they needed protection from eight mounted police and several N.Y.P.D. cruisers to depart the arena.

DOUG MOHNS

The left wing/defenseman who played for the Bruins from 1953 to 1964 had a trick he pulled on the opposition that was aggravating and led to a painful injury. When an opponent would drop his stick, Mohns would kick it away, forcing the player to chase it.

In December of 1958 in Chicago, Mohns kicked the stick of the Blackhawks' Ian Cushenan after a brief scuffle in which the big defenseman had dropped it. Not content to just give it one kick, Mohns kept kicking it farther and farther away, until the powerful Cushenan rushed at him and broke his jaw, putting him out of action for a month.

CAM NEELY

Cam celebrated his 21st birthday by learning of his trade to the Bruins for center Barry Pederson on June 6, 1986. The native of British Columbia and a boyhood friend of baseball's Larry Walker would be heading to the other side of the continent, and his career was poised for a real takeoff.

In a short time Cam became a beloved and respected member of the Bruins, all in part for his ability to score, his remarkable tenacity, and his potent fists. Midway through his first season in black and gold he managed his first career hat trick. In the spring of 1991, Cam became the Bruins' all-time leading playoff goal scorer. On November 4, 1993 he scored his 300th career goal. And on March 7, 1994, Neely scored his 50th goal of the season in only the 44th game, a feat only surpassed by Wayne Gretzky.

But it was a night in the late 1980s in a game versus the rival Canadiens that provided a real "Cam Neely moment." He had gotten in the way of an Allen Pedersen slap shot and required 16 stitches in his forehead. Not only did he come back out on the ice later in the game, he got into a fight with Shane Corson and completely opened the stitches up again. But Neely always played without regard for his own safety.

Fan favorite Cam Neely in the early 1990s.

By the late 1990s, after having to retire, Neely was playing with the likes of actor Jim Carrey instead of goalie Jim Carey, and made an appearance in the movie *Dumb and Dumber*. In Cam's scene, he was required to bust in a men's room stall with Carrey inside. The director was looking for a certain facial expression, and after a few takes, Cam wasn't quite capturing it. Finally, on one take, as Cam busted through the door, Carrey was inside giving him "the moon," although it was not seen on camera. This elicited the desired surprised facial expression from Cam.

New Hampshire Bruins

In the 1970s there was increasing talk of replacing the venerable old Boston Garden, which some felt had become a bit tired over the decades. One plan to build a new arena in the city's South Station area never materialized. Bruins management began to look not only outside of the city for a potential site, but out of state.

On January 16, 1981, the team publicly announced its intention to move to a proposed $50 million sports complex in Salem, N. H. As time went on, however, this plan, too, never came to pass, and it would be more than a decade before a new site would pop up—right in their own back yard.

CHRIS NILAN

In many ways, it almost seemed a natural that Chris Nilan would end up a Boston Bruin. Born in Boston on Dit Clapper's birthday, Chris almost seemed to have the Bruins' style of play ingrained in him long before he donned the black and gold.

One of "Knuckles's" most lasting contributions to Bruins' history in his relatively brief stay was setting the NHL record for most penalties in one game. In the final regular season game of 1991, Nilan was whistled for a total of 10 infractions in a 7-3 win over the rival Hartford Whalers.

JACK NORRIS

Regular Bruins goalie Eddie Johnston had just injured his hand on January 30, 1965, and Jack Norris was immediately promoted from the Los Angeles Blades of the Western Hockey League and was set to make his NHL debut.

Unfortunately, thieves intervened, stealing all of Norris's goalie equipment from the Royal York Hotel in Toronto, delaying his debut until the gear could be replaced. Norris made his debut the next night against the Maple Leafs back in Boston, wearing a very unusual number for a goalie, No, 17.

Norris went on to play 23 games for Boston that season, but ended up back down in the minor leagues until he was part of the famous Phil Esposito trade in May of 1967.

DENNIS O'BRIEN

When the defenseman was claimed on waivers from the Cleveland Barons on March 10, 1978, he became the first player to play for four NHL teams in a single season. Upon learning of yet another trade, he said, "I always wanted to play for a contender," but in the previous few years it seemed as though he had played for everything but. Though only 16 of the 64 games he played that season were with Boston, the only two goals he scored that season came in a Bruins uniform.

MIKE O'CONNELL

A second-generation professional athlete, O'Connell's father was a quarterback for the Cleveland Browns of the NFL back in the 1950s. Born in Chicago, Mike's family soon relocated to Massachusetts, where he grew up in the seaside town of Cohasset. He attended Archbishop Williams High School in Braintree, near Boston, where he was scouted as a young defenseman by Bruins scout Bill Tisdale. At the suggestion of Harry Sinden and Tom Johnson, Mike went to play hockey after high school in the Ontario Hockey League to gain valuable experience in Canadian Junior hockey.

O'Connell was ultimately drafted by the Blackhawks out of junior hockey in 1975, and went on to make his NHL debut with them in 1978. But in December of 1980, his hometown team came calling, shipping Al Secord to Chicago in exchange for him. Mike went on to play in the 1984 All-Star team as a member of the Bruins.

Since his retirement as an active player in 1990, he has served the Bruins as an assistant coach, coach of the top farm team in Providence, and was finally named to replace Harry Sinden as Bruins general manager on November 1, 2000. Sinden, who had played a role in O'Connell's early development as an aspiring NHL player had now played a role in his elevation to a top executive position.

FRED O'DONNELL

O'Donnell was playing right wing for the Bruins' top farm team, the Boston Braves, in their inaugural season when in a game versus the Cleveland Barons he got into a fight with Richie Leduc. Two weeks later, the Bruins acquired Leduc and immediately placed him on the same line as... Fred O'Donnell. The two forwards quickly buried the hatchet and both graduated up to the Bruins, where they were teammates for two seasons.

*   *   *

Fred O'Donnell and Bobby Orr were both married on September 8, 1973... but of course not to each other.

SEAN O'DONNELL

With defenseman O'Donnell's life, it is a case of "the NHL meets Hollywood." Sean's wife, actress Allison Dunbar, has appeared on numerous television shows as a guest star, including *Law and Order, C.S.I., Diagnosis: Murder, Silk Stalkings, Strip Mall,* and *Pacific Blue.*"

BILLY O'DWYER

It is a hockey story set almost entirely in Boston. Billy was born in Boston, grew up in the city's South Boston section, and played college hockey for Boston College for four years.

But it was with the Los Angeles Kings that he made his NHL debut, playing five games during the 1983-84 season. It was the following season that he netted his first NHL goal, and he couldn't have been more thrilled to reach the milestone right at home on Boston Garden ice.

O'Dwyer ultimately signed as a free agent with the Bruins on August 13, 1987, playing with the hometown team until 1990.

WILLIE O'REE

Though it isn't completely accurate to call O'Ree the "Jackie Robinson of hockey" as he has been referred to by some, it is significant that he was the first black player to skate in the history of the NHL. His relatively brief stay at hockey's top level began when he appeared in his first game with the Bruins on January 18, 1958. He only saw action in two games that season before being sent back down to the minors and didn't come back up until the 1960-61 season. He scored his first NHL goal in a 3-2 win over Montreal on New Year's Day of 1961. O'Ree played in 43 Bruins games that season.

What makes it all the more remarkable that he was able to compete in the NHL at all is that he was blind in one eye, a fact that was virtually unknown in his time with Boston. O'Ree had been hit in the right eye with a puck during his time in junior hockey with Kitchener in 1956. By the turn of the century, O'Ree had been hired by the NHL to work for its Diversity Task Force, traveling around the country working hard to interest inner-city children in careers in hockey.

Terry O'Reilly

An alumnus of Bobby Orr's junior hockey team, the Oshawa Generals, O'Reilly had joined the junior team three seasons after Orr departed for Boston. After three seasons with Oshawa, Terry began his pro career playing the 1971-72 season with the Bruins' top farm team, the Boston Braves. The following season he became a regular with the Bruins, but skating was clearly his weakness, and he tended to fall down quite often. Montreal coach Scotty Bowman observed early on, "He seems to have trouble skating for a big-leaguer." Bruins teammates gave him a pair of double-runner skates as a joke. *Boston Globe* sportswriter Ray Fitzgerald joked in February of 1973, "Terry O'Reilly hasn't learned how to keep from tripping over the blue line."

O'Reilly worked extremely hard on his skating during the next couple of years and improved enough to keep the pranksters off his back. Don Cherry said in December of 1978 that O'Reilly "made it on sheer guts and determination."

*   *   *

Long-time Boston hockey writer Tom Fitzgerald was one of the first in the media to realize what O'Reilly could mean to the Bruins in the long run, when a colleague accusingly claimed, "You just like him and write about him because his name is O'Reilly," to which Fitzgerald replied, "That's not true. I'd feel the same if his name were O'Brien."

Those who watched him throughout his career tend to regard Terry O'Reilly as the personification of what it meant to be a Boston Bruin. He possessed a work ethic that was a reflection of his adopted city, and helped the late 1970s edition of Bruins earn nicknames such as "the Lunchpail Athletic Club," or "the Blue Collar Gang." Yet there was quite a contrast to his on-ice and off-ice demeanors. O'Reilly greatly resented the reputation of being a "goon." While he would never avoid a confrontation in a hockey uniform, away from the rink he could be found shopping for antiques, or studying textbooks to educate himself. Terry was a straight-A student in high school, and in the summertime early in his career with the Bruins, he attended colleges such as the Universities of Toronto and Ottawa. In the summer of 1975 he took a course in calculus at Boston University.

*   *   *

106

Former Boston Bruins captain Terry O'Reilly, front, walks to the podium during ceremonies to have his number, 24, retired Thursday night, Oct. 24, 2002, in Boston. From left are former Bruins Bobby Orr, John Bucyk, Milt Schmidt and Ray Bourque, all of whose numbers have been retired.

"Taz" as he was known earned quite a distinction during the 1977-78 season when he became the first player in NHL history to amass more than 200 penalty minutes while also finishing in the top 10 scoring. But it is the penalties that O'Reilly tends to be remembered for, as he holds the career team record with 2,095 minutes. Throughout the course of his 13-year NHL career, spent entirely with Boston, he spent the equivalent of 35 games in the penalty box. At the "Last Hurrah" game, the final hockey event ever held at the Boston Garden, O'Reilly, Fernie Flaman, and Stan Jonathan fittingly posed for a photo together seated in the penalty box.

When the old Boston Garden was torn down in 1996, the penalty box was given to O'Reilly.

BOBBY ORR

If not for World War II, the Bruins may have had their first Orr suiting up for them back in the 1940s. Harold Cotton, chief scout for the Bruins at the time had observed Bobby's father, Doug, playing for the junior hockey Parry Sound Pilots, and had taken an interest in him and his teammate Pete Horeck. In 1941, he offered both the opportunity to sign on with the Bruins farm system, but Doug was intent on joining the navy. Many seemed to feel that Orr was the more skilled of the two players, particularly a better skater, but Horeck accepted the offer and went on to have an eight-year career in the NHL, two years of which were spent with Boston. Doug Orr came home from the navy and started a family in Parry Sound, but still had one very important contribution to make to the game of hockey.

Bobby Orr in his first training camp with the Bruins in the fall of 1966 sporting the unfamiliar No. 27.

Bobby became Bruins property in 1962 when he was just 14 years old. Milt Schmidt said that if Bobby had weighed 175 pounds at that time, he had the ability to play in the NHL right then. When it came time to negotiate a pro contract with the Bruins in the summer of 1966, Bobby's father Doug got the distinct impression that general manager Hap Emms was trying to lowball them with an offer of a $5,000 bonus and an $8,000 salary. Mr. Orr retained the services of agent Alan Eagleson, and after months of haggling, Bobby finally signed on September 3, 1966 for approximately $70,000 for two years. It was said that the signing of Orr indirectly led to the formation of the NHL Players' Association.

* * *

Shortly after Orr made his debut in the NHL, veteran superstar Gordie Howe admitted that he began to study Orr's technique for new ideas. At the NHL Awards ceremony after Orr's rookie season, New York Rangers defenseman Harry Howell, who had won the Norris Trophy as the league's best defenseman said, "I might as well enjoy it now. It's going to be Bobby Orr's for the next 10 years. I'm going to be the last guy to win it before they change it to the Bobby Orr Trophy."

* * *

An illustration of the character of young Bobby Orr came, when on at least two occasions early in his career he stopped to help people he did not know who were having trouble with their automobiles in the Boston Garden parking lot.

* * *

Bobby Orr in his prime, weaving his magic.

One of the Bruins' pranksters, Orr once secretly cut the bottom of Phil Esposito's socks. When Espo was dressing after the game, he pulled one of the socks almost up to his thigh as his teammates howled with laughter.

*   *   *

On one occasion at the Boston Garden when an opposing player was given a penalty for hooking Orr, a fan yelled to the referee, "Make that two and a half minutes. Two minutes for hooking, and an extra 30 seconds for hooking Bobby Orr!"

But likely the worst reaction by the Boston Garden crowd to an act against Orr came in the first game of the semi-final playoffs against Toronto on April 2, 1969. With 1:57 left in the second period, rookie defenseman Pat Quinn flattened Orr along the boards with a vicious elbow that appeared to be premeditated. Bobby was left in a heap on the ice and needed to be helped off as he was then taken to Massachussetts General Hospital for x-rays.

Quinn was assessed with a five-minute major penalty, and had to suffer the wrath of the Boston faithful as he entered the box. He was showered with debris, insults, and even threats, but when the glass around the penalty box was shattered, the police had to act quickly in order to prevent a full-fledged riot. Quinn had fought Orr earlier in the season, but now Bruins fans, ever protective of their hero, wanted blood. Quinn was quickly ushered back to the dressing room to safety. The *Boston Globe's* Ray Fitzgerald wrote of Quinn, "He couldn't have caused more trouble if he had stuffed a body in a North Station locker."

Orr had suffered a mild concussion and a minor neck

injury, but the Bruins had pummeled the Maple Leafs that day by the embarrassing margin of 10-0, en route to a four-game sweep in the series.

OSHAWA/NIAGARA FALLS GAME

Though Bobby Orr would not make his debut at Boston Garden in a Bruins uniform until October of 1966, the first two games he ever played on Garden ice are largely forgotten.

On December 5, 1964 and December 27, 1965, the Bruins had two of their Junior A affiliates, the Oshawa Generals and the Niagara Falls Flyers play each other in the Garden in order to showcase the team's amateur talent for the local fans. The first game featured Orr's teammate, Wayne Cashman, scoring two goals in Oshawa's 3-1 victory. But it was the second matchup in December of 1965 that seems even more noteworthy in retrospect. Coached by Bep Guidolin, Orr, Cashman, and their fellow Generals again faced a Niagara Falls team that included Derek Sanderson and Don Marcotte, each of whom had already made their NHL debuts in very brief appearances with Boston earlier that season. One of the main highlights witnessed by the nearly 5,800 at the Garden that evening was Orr, showing a glimpse of what was to come by scoring a goal, assisting on two others, and playing superb defense.

But one other incident that seems more noteworthy today is that midway through the first period, Bobby engaged in a fight with Sanderson, his future teammate and friend, with both receiving five-minute major penalties.

GEORGE OWEN

One of the more fascinating and well-rounded characters in Bruins history is defenseman George Owen, a member of Boston's first Stanley Cup-winning team of 1929. Born in Hamilton, Ontario, his family relocated to Newton, Massachussetts, just outside of Boston when George was a young boy. After graduating from Newton High School, he attended Harvard University, where he starred in hockey and football. In the Harvard-Yale football game in 1922, Owen ran back a punt 81 yards in Harvard's 10-3 victory.

He debuted with the Bruins in January of 1929, two months before their Stanley Cup victory over the New York Rangers. On February 11, 1932, he became the first U.S.-raised player to score a hat trick in the NHL. After his NHL career, he was involved in a variety of endeavors, including teaching at Milton Academy, coaching the Massachusetts Institute of Technology hockey team, and becoming involved in the shoe business. In 1949, Owen designed a special baseball shoe for Joe DiMaggio, who had been troubled by a bad heel.

In the mid-1960s when Owen was approximately 65 years old, he was seen playing ice hockey on a pond in Weston, Massachussetts. In a pickup game with young men 45 years his junior, the graceful, athletic, elderly gentleman was still displaying hockey ability that was head and shoulders above every other player on the ice.

BRAD PARK

Back in his days with the New York Rangers, Park was considered a bitter rival of the Bruins, and clearly not a favorite of faithful Boston fans. Brad focused much more negative attention on himself from Bostonians with the release of his book "Play the Man," released in January of 1972. In the book, Park was highly critical of several Bruin players, including Derek Sanderson, Ted Green, John McKenzie, and even Bobby Orr. Of McKenzie, Park said that he symbolized the "bush" style of Bruins play. He also called the Boston Garden a "zoo" that was old, shabby, and grubby, and that the fans acted like maniacs.

At the 1972 NHL All-Star game there was considerable tension between Park and Bruins players Orr, Esposito, and McKenzie in the East All-Stars dressing room. Many Boston players would also take runs at Park a few months later during the Stanley Cup Finals.

It was certainly a shock when Park came to Boston three and a half years later in a blockbuster trade. But the prospect of an Orr/Park pairing on defense was intriguing even to those who may have still held a grudge against the former rival. While the two superstar defensemen only played together a handful of times, Park went on to become a beloved member of the Bruins, reaching several milestones and having many memorable games. On March 17, 1979, he had four assists in the first period of a 4-2 win over Chicago. The following year he became only the second defenseman, along with Orr, to amass 500 career assists. And his overtime goal to eliminate Buffalo from the playoffs in April of 1983 is still fondly recalled as one of the most important Bruins goals of the 1980s.

*   *   *

Early in 1979 after knee surgery that had just been performed, Park had a light hearted way of looking at it, describing it as, "Just a stop at the garage... the man says 'what's the model number and the part... and starts looking for it."

LYNN PATRICK

A member of hockey's famous Patrick family, Lynn served as the Bruins' general manager from 1953 through 1964. His son Craig went on to a respectable career as a forward in the NHL and further made a name for himself as general manager for both the New York Rangers and Pittsburgh Penguins.

But in 1960 when Craig was a standout in bantam hockey in Massachusetts, his father made it clear that he would not have a future with the Bruins. Lynn remembered his own experience as a young player with the Rangers when his father, Lester, was the head man there and promoted his son to the big club. "I was never judged on my merit as a hockey player. The fans felt the only reason I made the Rangers was because my dad Lester was the big man."

Though Craig expressed an interest in a future with the Bruins and his father could have placed him on the team's reserve list, he was sent the next year to school in Montreal. From there he went on to have a brief trial with Montreal's AHL team, and debuted in the NHL with California in 1971.

Brad Park went from being immensely unpopular in Boston as a Ranger to being beloved as a Bruin.

JIM "SEAWEED" PETTIE

"Seaweed," who earned his colorful nickname due to his long, dark, scraggly hair was the backup goalie to Gerry Cheevers and Gilles Gilbert during the 1978-79 season. One game he would most like to forget was on March 15 of that season at Boston Garden when former Bruin Phil Esposito of the New York Rangers scored four goals against him in a 7-4 Boston loss—that is, until his next appearance on March 28 when Seaweed played the entire game against Buffalo and lost 9-2.

That put an end to his time with the Bruins and his NHL career.

P.O.W. LT. JOHN BERRIO

In 1944, Art Ross received a letter from an American serviceman who was being held in a prisoner of war camp in Germany. The letter asked, "Will you please save two Bruins playoff tickets for me? I'll pick them up as soon as I get back to Boston."

The author of the letter, Lt. John Berrio was not released until May of 1945, more than a month after the Bruins were eliminated from the playoffs by Detroit.

Thirty-eight years later, Berrio showed up at the Bruins' office with the newspaper clipping from a Boston paper from 1944 telling of his request and asked if he could be granted tickets to the Bruins' 1973 playoffs. Management was unsure what to do about the request and asked him to check back with them when the playoff schedule was set.

JOHNNY PIERSON

The steady, reliable right wing spent his entire 11-year career with the Bruins, but a decade after he hung up his skates in 1958, he became a household figure to a new generation of fans. In the late 1960s, Pierson became the color analyst for Bruins television broadcasts on Boston's channel 38. His broadcast partner of many years, Fred Cusick remembered decades later that when the station had first purchased the very expensive instant-replay machine, it was not available to the broadcasters, but only to the television viewing audience at home. Cusick recalled that Pierson's ability to dissect and analyze the play was so uncanny that having seen a particular play only once, as it occurred live, he could then repeat exactly what had happened for the home viewing audience while they were watching the replay—unaware that Pierson did not have access to the replay and was going strictly from memory.

JACQUES PLANTE

In his first season in the NHL in the 1952-53 season, Plante was part of a Canadiens team that defeated the Bruins in the Stanley Cup Finals. Twenty years later he was brought to the Bruins at the tail end of the '73 season for what would be his final stop in the NHL.

The 44-year-old goaltending legend was acquired by Boston on March 3, 1973, and in his first Bruins game he displayed the old magic, shutting out Chicago 4-0 at the Garden. Three weeks later he repeated the feat over the Rangers in Boston for what would be the final shutout of his career. He skated off the ice that afternoon with his trademark raised arms seen so many times after a stellar Plante performance. With a vintage Plante in net, many felt that the Bruins had a good chance to capture the Cup for a second year in a row.

But come the opening round of playoffs against the Rangers, Plante's great performances were a thing of the past. He was beaten in Game 1, 6-2, and again in Game 2, 4-2, in what would be his last appearance in an NHL game. Eddie Johnston took over in goal and won Game 3, 4-2, but the Bruins were eliminated in five games.

GEORGE PLIMPTON

In the summer of 1977, esteemed author George Plimpton approached the Bruins management and requested the opportunity to suit up as a goaltender to play briefly in an exhibition game, then write about his experience. Plimpton was no stranger to this concept, having played quarterback for the NFL's Detroit Lions in a preseason game in the mid-1960s that resulted in a movie and book entitled *Paper Lion*. Plimpton's intention was to write a piece for *Sports Illustrated* on what life was like as an NHL goalie.

The author attended Bruins training camp in Fitchburg, Massachussetts and received a crash course in the art of goaltending from Jim "Seaweed" Pettie. In the midst of the experiment, Harry Sinden said of George, "The guy has guts. The first time he came out on the ice he could barely stand up on skates. But he's improved. He still has a hard time getting up once he goes down, but he keeps on trying." Bruins players were also having fun firing shots past his head, just to throw a little scare into him.

Plimpton's moment of truth came on October 6, 1977, in a special five-minute exhibition held just before the start of a preseason game against the Philadelphia Flyers. Sporting the number "00" on his black Bruins jersey, George faced a total of five shots, only the first of which got by him. His Boston teammates wanted to be sure he faced a penalty shot, and promptly hauled down Reggie Leach intentionally to set the stage. But Plimpton was equal to the task, stopping a laughing Leach.

The gimmick resulted not only in a magazine article, but was also the subject in a book years later entitled *Open Net.*

BABE PRATT

A great defenseman, Pratt concluded his 12-year NHL career with the Bruins in the 1946-47 season. He went on to be elected to the Hockey Hall of Fame, despite the fact that he had been suspended for gambling on games in late January of 1946. He was reinstated 17 days later.

Three years before Babe came to the Bruins, one of his gambling incidents that took its place in NHL lore occurred just before a game against Boston. The Bruins were forced to use a spare goalie due to their regular netminder being unavailable. In warmups, Pratt observed that the Bruins' spare goalie seemed incredibly slow and was barely able to stop the easiest of shots.

At that time, Pratt immediately went back to the Toronto locker room. He removed his skates, put on shoes, and threw on an overcoat over his uniform. He then walked up to a section of Maple Leaf Gardens where gamblers were known to congregate, and bet $500 on Toronto to win. The Maple Leafs did in fact win the contest by the surprisingly close score of 7-4.

JEAN PUSIE

One of the more colorful and downright eccentric players to ever appear in the NHL, Pusie seemed to be more of an entertainer than a hockey player. Aside from his brief stay as a defenseman with the Bruins during the 1934-35 season, he also had stints as a prize fighter and a professional wrestler.

One of his more noteworthy stunts in a game came when he was the only player back on a three-on-one break when he seemed to simply panic, throwing his stick up in the air and covering his eyes.

It is not hard to understand why a hockey purist like Art Ross did not keep him around long.

BILL QUACKENBUSH

The defenseman was such a gentlemanly player, he picked up only four minutes in penalties while playing in all 70 games of the 1955-56 season, but oddly enough did not win the Lady Byng Trophy. Perhaps after getting no penalties over the entire

1948-49 season while winning the trophy with Detroit, it was felt that he was becoming "chippy" in his old age.

RENE RANCOURT

Rene has become a recognized member of the Bruins family since he became the pregame national anthem singer for the team in 1976. A trained opera singer, he was born in Lewiston, Maine to parents who were born in Montreal, yet he had never been to a hockey game until he sang for the Bruins.

Rene was discovered in the early 1970s by organist John Kiley, who was well-known for having played regularly at Bruins, Celtics, and Red Sox games. Kiley heard Rancourt on a Boston radio show after he had won a New England Metropolitan Opera contest, and asked him if he would sing the national anthem at the opening game of the season for the Red Sox. Rene was repeatedly invited back, performing the anthem for Red Sox opening days for seven straight years. Kiley later asked him if he would do the anthem for a Bruins game. Rancourt had no idea where the Boston Garden was located and needed to ask directions to find it.

After he had performed the anthem at his first Bruins game, he realized he had entered a new world. He couldn't believe the enthusiasm displayed by the fans, particularly those who were pounding on the glass near ice level.

Two of his signature moves at the conclusion of his performance are the salute and the fist pump. Rene explains: "Many, many years ago, an elderly woman called me up and told me that she loved the way I performed the anthem. She said she wasn't a hockey fan, but that she turned it on to hear me sing, then turned it off. I told her I'd give her a salute the next time, and I just kept it up." As for the fist pump, Rene adopted it from diminutive left winger Randy Burridge, also known as "Stump," in the late 1980s. When Burridge scored a goal, he would do a fist pump that became known as the "Stump pump."

Among his more noteworthy memories singing at the old Boston Garden is having sung the Russian national anthem before a Soviet team played there. As he concluded the song, Soviet players began banging their sticks on the ice in approval. One of the more touching moments was singing "Auld Lang Syne" as former Bruin Normand Leveille was helped around the Garden ice on skates.

One forgettable night was when Rene forgot a few of the words to the anthem and had to mumble his way through. The following day, a Boston reporter wrote that Rancourt "Doo-bee-Dooed" his way through it, sounding a bit like Frank Sinatra.

JEAN RATELLE

When the classy center announced his retirement as a player in May of 1981, teammate Brad Park said of Ratelle, "It's amazing, really, that he was able to play the game. That might be the most amazing thing about Jean Ratelle's career—that such a tranquil man could play such an aggressive game and survive." Former teammate Rod Gilbert added, "In all the games we played, in all the practices, in all the time I've known him, I don't think I've ever heard Jean Ratelle swear. Not once. Never." In his newspaper column, Leigh Montville wrote, "On an ice surface filled with Marx Brothers madness and Three Stooges shenanigans, he was Fred Astaire in full glide."

Ratelle had a rather interesting choice of breakfast food, something a bit different from the typical bacon and eggs and such. He had a habit of taking several types of cereal, such as shredded wheat, corn flakes, rice crispies, etc., and mixing them in one bowl and putting sliced bananas on top—Jean's own "breakfast of champions!"

DAVE REECE

After playing goalie for the University of Vermont and spending a few years in the Bruins' farm system, including a two-season stint with the Boston Braves of the AHL, Reece was finally ready to make his NHL debut at the age of 27. In what would turn out to be his only season in the league, 1975-76, he appeared in just 14 games for the Bruins. It was his last game that should be the most forgettable, yet it is the only one that is ever recalled in the brief career of Dave Reece.

The Bruins were in Toronto for a game against the Maple Leafs on February 7, 1976. Gerry Cheevers had just returned from the WHA, Gilles Gilbert was set to return from an injury, and Reece was scheduled to be sent back down to Springfield in the minor leagues. He had just beaten Pittsburgh 5-1 in the last Bruins game two nights before, and Coach Cherry was going to give him one more start.

It was in that game that Leafs center Darryl Sitler erupted for six goals and four assists off Reece in an 11-4 drubbing. He was dubbed after as "The Human Sieve." This would go on to be Reece's final, lasting memory of life as a goaltender in the NHL.

Reunion of 1970 Stanley Cup Team

In May of 1990, Bobby Orr and others arranged to have a 20-year reunion of all of the members of the Bruins' 1970 Stanley Cup winning team. The Bruins were in the Stanley Cup Finals versus Edmonton at the time, and the proposed get-together was to take place after the conclusion of the series.

The Bruins ultimately lost that series to the Oilers, and the reunion was held on June 1, 1990 at the Guest Quarter Suite Hotel in Waltham, Massachussetts It was also felt that it would be a nice addition to have the Stanley Cup on hand for the event, but the Cup at that time was in possession of the newly crowned champion Oilers. It just so happened that Ted Green was an assistant coach on that Oilers team. Green, who would be attending the reunion, approached Oilers captain Mark Messier to ask if the Cup could be borrowed for the event for a couple of days. Messier announced to the team that Bobby Orr needed to borrow the Cup, and if anyone had any problems to come see him. No one had a problem with that.

Green said after that a terrific time was had by all at the well-attended affair, and that if all the guys had memories that good back in high school they would have all turned out to be Einsteins.

BOBBY RING

The NHL career of goaltender Bobby Ring came so early and went so fast he barely knew what had happened. With no professional experience and only one season in junior hockey, the 19-year-old Ring was being carried as the Bruins' spare goalie early in the 1965-66 season.

On October 30, 1965, Eddie Johnston had been injured midway through the second period in a game versus the Rangers at Boston Garden. Young Bobby was brought in to finish the game and allowed four goals in an 8-2 loss to New York.

In all, his NHL career lasted 33 minutes, as he was never seen in another game.

BRIAN ROLSTON

The center from Flint, Michigan was a member of the U.S. Olympic hockey team in 1994. Rolston came to the Bruins from Colorado in the Ray Bourque trade on March 6, 2000. Four months before he had been traded to the Avalanche from the New Jersey Devils in exchange for Claude Lemieux. Sportswriter Michael Holley of the *Boston Globe* wrote that Rolston had been traded for one player Bruins fans despised and another that they loved.

ART ROSS

To many fans, the name "Art Ross" is mainly associated with the trophy awarded to the player who leads the league in points each season. But it would be almost impossible to measure his impact on not only the Boston Bruins franchise, but the entire National Hockey League.

Probably no one man has meant more to the Bruins since the team's inception in 1924. It was he who instilled the trademark Bruin toughness and aggressive play right from the beginning, which carried on through the decades. As the Boston general manager right up until 1954, he was responsible for every player to wear the Bruins sweater for the team's first 30 years.

Ross was known to hockey buffs in Boston as far back as 1911, six years before the formation of the NHL when he came to the city with the Montreal Wanderers to engage in tournament play. He was one of Canada's finest players at the time, and had built up such a reputation as a great hockey man in subsequent years that when Charles Adams needed a man to run his new team in 1924, Ross was his choice.

Ross was an innovator without equal, and within his first two decades in the NHL he had redesigned the net, changing it to the "B"-shaped net still in use today; he had redesigned the puck, giving it its beveled edges; he had designed the first helmet; and he was the first coach to pull the goalie for a sixth attacker, which he did on March 26, 1931.

The "dour Scot" as he was known because of his gloomy, sullen demeanor, had a legendary feud with Toronto's legendary coach Conn Smythe. On December 13, 1932, the two

Art Ross—the man who is more responsible for Bruins history as it is than any other.

men got into a fight behind the bench during a Bruins-Leafs game that had to be broken up by police.

All in all, if there were one member of the Bruins organization who could be named its all-time MVP, Art Ross would indisputably be the man.

DEREK SANDERSON

The "Turk" will go down as one of the more flamboyant figures in the history of the Bruins franchise. Off the ice his flashy, playboy style was cast from the same mold as that of his friend "Broadway" Joe Namath of football's New York Jets. In the late 1960s and early 1970s, much attention was paid to his fancy clothes, his extravagant automobiles, and his posh bachelor apartment in one of Boston's exclusive neighborhoods. Along with former Red Sox player Ken Harrelson, a flamboyant type himself, and Patriots receiver Jim Colclaugh, Derek became part owner of a popular Boston nightclub known as "Bachelors III," and also by the early '70s had appeared in a Hollywood movie and hosted his own Boston-area talk show. *The Derek Sanderson Show*, which aired on local television featured Harry Nillson's "Everybody's Talkin' at Me" as its opening theme song. Among his more celebrated guests was a young recording sensation named Linda Ronstadt, singing her first solo hit "Long, Long Time."

Around that time, Derek had mentioned that he might bring his sense of fashion to his hockey uniform by wearing a custom pair of white skates, influenced by the white football shoes worn by Namath. Although he never went through with it, Bruins teammates threatened to secretly paint Derek's skates white. Sanderson had also raised eyebrows around the league in 1971 by being the first NHL player since the 1940s to wear a moustache.

Not to be overlooked is that the center from Niagara Falls, Ontario was a tremendous forechecker, penalty killer, and one of the league's finest face-off men. In his prime, he claimed to have won 38 face-offs in one particular game while only losing one.

At the Bruins training camp in September of 1967, Phil Esposito, Teddy Green, and Eddie Shack took the 21-year-old Sanderson out for a walk one day to try to convince him that he could make the team. They told him to keep his cockiness, but to also keep his cool. It was clear at that time that the young center was not going to be pushed around, and he proved quickly that he would drop the gloves and square off with anyone. In that rookie year of 1967-68 he fought the Rangers Orland Kurtenbach to a draw, and many took notice, as the rugged New York center was one of the best fighters in the league.

*   *   *

One of the most notorious incidents Sanderson was involved in on the ice with the Bruins came in Game 3 of the semi-final playoffs against the New York Rangers on April 11, 1970.

The Bruins had won the first two games in Boston, and the series had moved on to New York. A desperate Rangers team employed the strategy that if they could goad Sanderson into a fight and get him out of the game as early as possible, they would be rid of a thorn in their side and stood a better chance of winning. One minute and twenty seconds into the game, Sanderson was about to take a faceoff in the New York end, and goalie Ed Giacomin skated over to him and according to Derek said, "We are getting paid to get you," to which Sanderson replied, "Groovy... why don't you do it, big shot?" Eleven seconds later when he went in the corner to get the puck, both Walt Tkaczuk and Arnie Brown charged at him, and a melee ensued. Derek ended up fighting both Brown and Dave Balon, and was given a major penalty for fighting, a 10-minute misconduct, and an automatic game misconduct. Of New York's strategy, Sanderson said later, "As far as I'm concerned, this is the greatest compliment that could ever be paid to me." The Rangers did win the game 4-3, but the Bruins had the last laugh by winning the series in six games on their way to their Stanley Cup victory. They also needed a police escort to leave Madison Square Garden the night of the Sanderson ambush.

*　　*　　*

When the Bruins won the Stanley Cup against the Rangers in New York, Boston's Logan Airport was mobbed to greet them upon their return. In order to slip past the maddening crowd, Derek borrowed a mechanic's uniform and cap, got a ride from the plane in a baggage truck, then walked past thousands almost completely unnoticed.

*　　*　　*

A month after the Bruins won the Stanley Cup in 1972, Sanderson accepted an enormous offer from the Philadelphia Blazers of the brand new World Hockey Association that was to pay him $2.6 million for 10 years. Among his many purchases at that time was a 28-room mansion with a full-time maid and valet.

Derek appeared in a grand total of eight games for Philadelphia. He injured his back three weeks into his first season, and never suited up for the team after their November 1 game against Gerry Cheevers's Cleveland Crusaders. Sanderson and the team finally parted ways in late January of 1973, as he received a reported $1 million buyout of his WHA contract. On February 7, 1973 through his agent Bob Woolf, Derek agreed to return to the Bruins for $200,000 for the remainder of the 1973 season, as well as the 1973-74 season. Upon his return to Boston, Sanderson was believed to be the only NHL player who drove a Rolls-Royce. But though he had no shortage of buying power, one thing he didn't seem interested in buying was his old uniform number 16. Bruins rookie right wing Fred O'Donnell offered the number back for $2,000, but was turned down.

*   *   *

Derek had made his first foray into the movie business with a walk-on role in a movie that was filmed in August of 1970 called *Loving and Laughing*. Because of its content, the filmed earned an X-rating, but Sanderson, only on screen for approximately 90 seconds, remained clothed and did not partake in the activities. His role was as a scout for a girls hockey team.

Derek Sanderson—one of the more colorful players in Bruins history.

The movie had played in Canada, but when it was about to be distributed in the United States early in 1972, Derek asked the producers for his scene to be deleted, which they agreed to do. Shortly before the movie opened in Boston, several local reporters did get to view the version that included Derek, and they felt that as an actor he was a good hockey player.

*   *   *

Shortly after Sanderson was traded to the rival New York Rangers on June 12, 1974, he met with reporters in the Rangers' dressing room. He mentioned that he thought it was time to dispose of his Rolls-Royce, probably in favor of a Jaguar. When he was reminded by new teammate Brad Park that management requires the players to wear neckties, Derek replied, "No problem. I must have a lot of them in a closet somewhere." He also said that in a short time the Bruins would deeply regret trading him more than any deal they had made in the previous 10 years. He gave a parting shot to Bruins ownership, saying, "All those Storer Broadcasting people know about hockey could be printed on the head of a pin in black type." Sanderson never really was a force again in the league however, playing for four different teams in his final four seasons.

Terry Sawchuk

Of all the great players to have performed in the National Hockey League, Sawchuk may well be one of the most enigmatic, and appeared to have been plagued by more than his share of personal problems. When Bruins general manager Lynn Patrick was discussing trade possibilities with Jack Adams of the Detroit Red wings in the spring of 1955, the two men agreed in principle that Detroit would include a goalie in the deal, though no specific name was mentioned. Patrick had assumed that Adams was likely referring to Glen Hall, who had yet to establish himself as a regular in the NHL. As talks progressed, Patrick was stunned to find out that Sawchuk was the goalie he would receive and quickly agreed to the deal.

In time, it became clear that Sawchuk came with a bit of baggage. He could be a man who was extremely moody, experiencing joyous highs and deep, dark lows. As a member of the Bruins, he rented a large home in Newton, Massachussetts that he shared with teammates Jerry Toppazzini, Doug Mohns, Don McKenney, and Lionel Heinrich. The agreement between the roommates was that they would share the household chores evenly, but many times Sawchuk would come home after a game or practice and withdraw into a shell. He would sit at the kitchen table and chain smoke in an almost trance-like state, speaking to no one for hours at a time. Many seemed to also feel that he was greatly depressed from being separated from his wife and children, who were living back in the Detroit area, yet even his wife would later describe him as being extremely difficult to deal with on game days.

Sawchuk performed quite well with Boston, and often

amazed the Garden crowd with his breathtaking saves. Midway through the 1956-57 season, his second with the Bruins, he had suffered a variety of ailments, including mononucleosis, that caused him to be hospitalized for a couple of weeks. Very shortly after he was named to the NHL All-Star team, he announced to the world that he was through with hockey and boarded a train for his home in Michigan. Days after his arrival, his doctor announced that Sawchuk was on the verge of a complete nervous breakdown.

He would never suit up for the Bruins again, and that July he was traded back to Detroit in the deal that brought John Bucyk to Boston.

BOBBY SCHMAUTZ

Hockey players are known for their ability to withstand pain and punishment, yet they do have their limits. In December of 1978, right wing Schmautz suffered an eye injury and broke his nose in three places. After allowing doctors to reset the nose without anesthesia, he stated emphatically, "I guarantee I'll never let them do that to me again."

*   *   *

In the late 1970s, coach Don Cherry became aware before a game that Schmautz had a terrific hangover from excessive revelry the night before. During the game, Cherry thought he'd teach Bobby a lesson and give him more playing time than he cared to have on that particular night, serving time on power plays and penalty-killing situations as well as his regular shifts. Cherry could see that his tactic was effective as Schmautz's tongue was hanging out as the game progressed.

Imagine Cherry's surprise when Bobby scored the winning goal on a breakaway late in the third period.

MILT SCHMIDT

Those younger fans who came to know Milt as an older, distinguished, gray-haired gentleman have difficulty at first realizing the true magnitude of the toughness he displayed as a hockey player. Known as an extremely tough body-checker, he once said, "I can't help it if these guys just keep running into my elbows." Later in his career he often was plagued with injuries, including troublesome knees. In 1951, Bruins trainer Hammie Moore said that he used 18 feet of tape on Schmidt's bad knee before every game that season. Until Orr came along, Schmidt was very likely the second most popular Bruin behind only Eddie Shore. Until Esposito arrived, he was undoubtedly the franchise's best center. Art Ross called him the best all-around player he ever saw.

When Schmidt first arrived at the Boston Arena to play with the Bruins, none other than Eddie Shore attempted to change Milt's skating style right away. Shore favored a straight, standing-up position, and observed that Schmidt skated much more bent over. He told him if he didn't change his style, he'd never make it in the NHL. When Schmidt mentioned this to veteran Dit Clapper, whom Milt would say later treated him like a son, Clapper told him not to change anything and to stick with what got him there.

Milt Schmidt, sporting his Bruins coaching sweater in the late 1950s.

When Milt retired as a player in 1954, Boston sportswriter D. Leo Monahan wrote that trainer Moore "took jersey number 15, folded it carefully and placed it next to three others in a sacrosanct section of a little-used equipment trunk."

* * *

When Schmidt served as Bruins general manager during their Stanley Cup-winning season of 1969-70, he had the pleasure of being in possession of the Cup for one entire day after the team's victory in the Finals. He and his wife weren't quite sure what to do with the coveted trophy, but finally decided to put it in a baby's crib and tuck it in for a good night's sleep.

EDDIE SHACK

Few who witnessed the incident will likely ever forget it. On March 7, 1968, the Bruins were playing the Philadelphia Flyers at, of all places, Toronto's Maple Leaf Gardens. The Flyers' arena, the Spectrum, had incurred damage to its roof, and a few of their games had to be scheduled in neutral site NHL facilities.

That night, Bruins left wing Eddie Shack became involved in a lengthy, dangerous, and bloody stick fight with the Flyers' Larry Zeidel. Each player received cuts on his face and head that required several stitches to close. Shack would say later that the two had a feud that went back about 10 years when they played in the American Hockey League. The two had a stick fight at that time as well and were ejected from the game.

Both players dressed and went into the stands to watch the rest of the game, but they resumed their slugfest there and had to be separated by local police.

Sean Shanahan

When forward Sean Shanahan made his Bruins debut in Boston on December 4, 1977, his misspelled name on the back of his jersey raised fewer eyebrows than another aspect of the uniform. Aside from being identified on the sweater as "SHANANAHAN," the young player recently called up from Rochester was sporting popular Phil Esposito's former No. 7. No player had worn the number since Espo departed two years before.

Issuing the number to such a nondescript player as Shanahan would seem to place unnecessary attention on him, and he was indeed the target of a few comments from the crowd. Some even felt it may have been intended as a bit of a zing at Phil from Bruins management. On receiving the number, Shanahan said, "I'm honored. The only thing is, Phil and I play totally different styles."

Indeed. Shanahan played a total of six games for the Bruins and had a career total of one goal.

The "Shave"

In the 1960s, the Bruins team engaged in a somewhat bizarre rookie-hazing ritual, the details of which are not quickly revealed by victims, witnesses, or participants.

A handful of veteran players would surround an unsuspecting rookie during training camp, oftentimes in a hotel room, and the fun would begin. The poor victim would be restrained and stripped down, and would be shaved from head to toe with a dry razor.

If it was not so humorous in an odd sort of a way, it would almost be disturbing.

STEVE SHIELDS

By the time the 30-year-old goaltender had come to the Bruins, he had seen considerable experience in the NHL with both the Buffalo Sabres and San Jose Sharks. In training camp with Boston for the first time in the fall of 2002, Steve was exposed to Bruins part-time goalie coach and consultant Gerry Cheevers.

After having the chance to work with the Hall of Fame goalie, Shields decided to pay tribute to him by having his goalie mask painted with stitches all over it, reminiscent of the mask Cheevers made famous.

EDDIE SHORE

The stellar defenseman known as the "Edmonton Express" may forever remain the prime example of the tough, brutal iceman from the great white north. The numerous accounts of his almost ridiculous ability to not only dish out punishment, but to receive it in phenomenal quantities are legendary in the world of hockey, and many bear repeating here. During his career, he had his nose broken 14 times, his jaw broken five times, had all of his teeth knocked out, and received a total of just under 1,000 stitches. He has been referred to as "the Ty Cobb of hockey," in part due to his utterly relentless desire to win, his maniacal desire to prove his toughness, and the passionate feelings, both good and bad, that were held for him by fans throughout the league. Shore was regarded as the biggest drawing card in the NHL in the 1920s and '30s, and many fans in opposing cities came to the arena in hopes of seeing him get maimed. On a few occasions, they did.

The punishment Shore withstood began almost immediately after donning a Bruins sweater for the first time. In his first training camp in the fall of 1926, he was competing for a spot on defense with "Wild" Billy Coutu, a brutally rugged backliner who had just been acquired from the Canadiens.

Coutu picked up a loose puck and came charging up the ice with a full head of steam in Shore's direction. As the veteran lowered his head, Shore didn't back off, and the two defensemen met head-on. Shore didn't budge, remaining on his feet as Coutu bounced off and was knocked out and missed a week of action. It was quickly noticed that Shore's ear was split from top to bottom, with half of it hanging on virtually by a thread. At first he told the attending doctor to simply snip it off and sew up the wound, but he was able to stitch the ear back together—with Shore holding up a hand mirror to watch the procedure, giving instructions all the while.

Shore was back on the ice as a regular the next day.

In his second season, Boston was in Montreal to face the Maroons, the City's english-speaking NHL representatives. Great Hall of Fame defenseman Red Dutton, Babe Siebert, one of Shore's chief rivals, and company decided to test his toughness. They worked Shore over viciously, and by game's end he had gashes over and under both eyes, had two teeth knocked out, and also had a broken nose. It also bears mentioning that he played the entire 60 minutes of the game and scored two goals. He was taken to the hospital after the game for observation, but after a short time he grabbed his clothes and left. Again, he was in the lineup the next game.

One of the more often-repeated Shore incidents came in January of 1929. He had missed the team's train to Montreal to play the Maroons the following night and, though the entire northeast was expecting a blizzard, he decided to rent a limousine to drive him all the way.

As expected, the snowstorm made driving conditions horrible, and several times the car went off the road. Shore finally told the driver to move over as he jumped behind the wheel. The utterly harrowing trip took 22 hours as Shore arrived in Montreal an hour before game time with hardly a wink of sleep. Though he appeared to be in no shape to play, he was on the ice for the entire game and scored the only goal in the Bruins' 1-0 victory.

Shore once received a large gash from a skate blade between his eyes and was carried unconscious to the bench. There he was revived and the trainer closed the cut with a large piece of tape and Shore skated back out on the ice and resumed playing.

But the most well-known incident regarding Eddie Shore has been the Ace Bailey incident that occurred in a game against the Toronto Maple Leafs on December 12, 1933. The Bruins and Leafs were bitter rivals, seemingly always feuding, and on this particular night there had already been several brawls. Boston had a two-man advantage and as Shore was making one of his patented rushes up the ice with the puck, he got checked very hard against the boards by King Clancy. The bone-rattling check made Shore hit his head and he collapsed in a heap on the ice. When he was finally able to collect himself and climb to his feet, he charged the nearest Toronto player in a rage and cross-checked him in the lower back. The player happened to be 30-year-old right winger Irvine "Ace" Bailey, who flipped up in the air and came crashing down on his head with a sickening thud that was heard throughout the Garden. Immediately afterwards, Toronto's Red Horner reacted by throwing a punch at Shore that knocked him to the ice and split his head open, leaving him in a pool of blood. The Bruin defenseman was carried off the ice and required 16 stitches, while Bailey was rushed to the hospital, where for the next two weeks he lay near death. It was reported that Bailey's father came to Boston with a gun looking for Shore.

Bailey miraculously recovered, though he was not able to resume his career as a hockey player. He actually lived to the ripe old age of 88. Shore was punished by the league with a 16-game suspension. Three months after the incident, on February 14, 1934, an all-star game was held in Toronto to benefit Bailey. That night, he and Shore met for the first time since the incident and shook hands at center ice in an extremely dramatic moment.

*   *   *

The incomparable Eddie Shore.

Shore was known to be supremely confident in his abilities and was not afraid to taunt opponents with that confidence. In the late 1920s, he was known to skate out on the Garden ice as the team was being announced wearing a matador's cape, followed by an assistant who would remove the cape. On another occasion he skated out onto the ice wearing a bathrobe, signifying that he could beat the opposition after just crawling out of bed.

*   *   *

In the late 1920s the New York Rangers cast their eyes towards Shore and made a trade proposal in which they offered defenseman Myles Lane (a Boston area native who was later sold to the Bruins) for him. Coach Art Ross sent a telegram back to Ranger management that read simply, "You are so many Myles from Shore you need a life preserver."

A decade later, Shore did end up in New York, playing for the city's other NHL team, the Americans. By the 1939-40 season he had become a bit disillusioned with Bruins management and made a move that prompted the team to dispose of him. He had purchased the Springfield Indians of the American Hockey League and asked the Bruins if he could split time playing for both teams. They objected to the request and shipped him to the Americans on January 25, 1940 for Ed Wiseman and $5,000 as the Eddie Shore era came to a close in Boston.

* * *

In 1941 with Canada becoming involved in World War II, Shore offered a General in the Royal Canadian Air Force $35,000 to give him a chance to become a fighter pilot, which was rejected.

* * *

In 1945, Shore was still regarded by many historians and analysts as the greatest player to have played in the NHL. Yet when he was asked that year to write a book about hockey, he gave a surprisingly modest answer, saying, "I am considering it, and expect to write a book in a few years—when I know enough about hockey. I am finding out new things every game and sometimes I have to change my ideas."

*   *   *

When Shore was still coaching his Springfield team in the AHL in the early 1960s, most who saw him conducting practices believed that even at 60 years old, he could still skate better than most players It even appeared that he could skate faster backwards than most of his players could forward.

HARRY SINDEN

Sinden had been promoted by the Bruins to take over as the team's coach after serving as the coach of their top farm team in Oklahoma City. That first season in Boston did not go particularly well, despite the presence of rookie Bobby Orr. The Bruins ended up in last place, missing the playoffs for the eighth straight year. One time a vocal fan at the Garden hollered out, "Hey Sinden, there's a bus leaving soon for Oklahoma City. Be under it!"

*   *   *

Many remember that when Orr scored his famous winning goal to make Sinden a Stanley Cup-winning coach in 1970, St. Louis defenseman Noel Picard was the one to trip Orr to send him flying through the air. Few remember, however, that it was the rugged Picard who broke Sinden's jaw in four places with one punch in a minor-league game seven years earlier.

*   *   *

Harry Sinden in his first year behind the Bruins bench, 1966-67.

Everyone was shocked when four days after winning the Stanley Cup in May of 1970, 37-year-old coach Sinden announced he was leaving the team and the NHL to take a job in private industry. He had been making $17,500 per year, and Bruins president Weston Adams Jr. stated that he had offered him a raise of $5,000. Sinden would claim that he had made up his mind to leave hockey two days before the previous Christmas, 1969, and would have left even if the Bruins had not won the Cup. Every Bruins player who was asked expressed their surprise and had kind words for their ex-coach.

Harry took a job with a company in Rochester, N.Y. called Sterling Homex owned by a childhood friend that produced pre-fabricated housing. He thought it represented a tremendous opportunity, but unfortunately the business went bankrupt within two years. Sinden was asked to coach Team Canada in a series against Russia, and his team of NHL stars captured the series in dramatic fashion. He returned as Bruins general manager in October of 1972, a position he would hold for more than 25 years.

DALLAS SMITH

The Gallery Gods certainly must have taken notice of a rather Eddie Shore-like incident involving Smith, the tough Manitoba farmer. After taking a puck in the mouth and having several teeth knocked out as a result, he came back out on the ice to play the next period.

*   *   *

Smith's teammates in the early 1970s called him "Half-Ton," but it had nothing to do with his size. In every city that the team would visit on the road, he would search the local truck dealers for half-ton trucks for his father's farm.

JIM STEWART

The native of Cambridge, Massachussetts, right next door to Boston, got the chance to live the dream when he appeared in net for his home team in 1980. Unfortunately, the dream quickly turned to a nightmare that lasted a grand total of 20 minutes.

Stewart played goal for one ghastly period and let in five goals. As the horrible period was coming to a close for the shell-shocked local boy, a statement was made by an extremely insensitive and opinionated fan to general manager Harry Sinden for all to hear. As a hush came over the Garden, the lone voiced called out in a sing-song voice "Har-ry... he su-ucks!"

Poor Mr. Stewart never cast his shadow over the Bruins goal crease again.

BOB SWEENEY

The forward, who was born in Concord, Massachussetts played high school hockey at nearby Acton-Boxboro High School and was a teammate there of future NHL star goalie Tom Barrasso for three years. Barrasso was signed by the Buffalo Sabres after graduating, while Sweeney played hockey at Boston College for four years. Bob then signed with the Bruins, and made his NHL debut in January of 1987.

In his second NHL game, on January 26, Sweeney scored his first NHL goal, remarkably against his old teammate Tom Barrasso!

JOE THORNTON

In his very early days with the Bruins, 6'4", 225-pound Joe could be viewed as a bit of a man-child. On one hand he was a physically mature young man on the threshold of greatness, earning an executive-like base salary of $925,000 per year. At the same time he was a teenager who wore "Scooby Doo" cartoon underwear and boarded with a family in nearby Brookline, Massachussetts.

Joe Thornton

Jerry Toppazzini

The right winger was an effective scoring threat for the Bruins in the mid-1950s, but was never more effective than on the night of December 16, 1956. "Topper" scored two goals in 10 seconds to help beat the Maple Leafs 4-2.

Four years later he got a goalie's view of the game very briefly. In October of 1960, Bruins goalie Don Simmons was injured very late in the game, and Jerry went in to fill in for him, becoming the last position player to ever appear in goal in an NHL game.

Carol Vadnais

The Bruins acquired outstanding defenseman Vadnais from the California Golden Seals on February 23, 1972, and relieved him of the embarrassment of wearing white skates. On his first trip to Philadelphia as a member of the Bruins to play the Flyers the following December, he got into a fight with a fan at the Spectrum and was taken to the police station in a paddy wagon. The fan turned out to be a retired army colonel who decided to press charges.

During his next trip to Philadelphia, Vadnais was mistaken for a bank robber and taken into custody. As he was being led away from the hotel by the authorities, he looked at Eddie Johnston and said, "Eddie, tell them who I am. Tell them I'm a hockey player!" Johnston hesitated just long enough to allow the police to take him away. The bank teller was finally able to tell police that he wasn't the hold-up man.

*   *   *

In the early 1970s, there was a popular movie in the theaters called *Bob and Carol and Ted and Alice*. After Vadnais came to the Bruins, the defensive corps came to be referred to as "Bob, Carol, Ted and Dallas" — for Orr, Vadnais, Green, and Smith.

JOE WATSON

During the 1964-65 season, Watson was in the Bruins' farm system, playing defense for Minneapolis. While the Bruins were on a road trip in Chicago, they happened to be short of defensemen, and G.M. Lynn Patrick put out the call for Joe to join the team for the Blackhawks game that evening. When Watson discovered there were no commercial flights available, team owner Weston Adams Sr. arranged to have a chartered flight bring him to Chicago in time for the game. Adams had on occasion been criticized for not caring enough about winning, because he was drawing great crowds and making money, but this incident helps to illustrate that he cared very deeply about what was best for the Bruins.

As for Watson, he ended up playing four games with Boston that season, but never made it back to the team before being claimed by the Philadelphia Flyers in the expansion draft in June of 1967. He went on to be a very solid defensive defenseman for the Flyers for the next decade.

JOHN WENSINK

When left winger Wensink came to the Bruins he had a reputation as merely a "goon" and a "policeman," but also became a favorite of the Garden's Gallery Gods. In his first two seasons in Boston, John had very modest scoring totals, but showed considerable improvement during the 1978-79 season. After scoring the winning goal in a 3-2 win over the Rangers on December 3, 1978, *Boston Globe* sportswriter John Ahern wrote "Wensink scored the winner, and if there is a more unlikely hero in the entire National Hockey League, his identity is unknown to man."

A week and a half later, Wensink surprised all, especially Ahern, by scoring the first hat trick of his career—a "natural" trick in a 7-3 win over Vancouver at the Boston Garden. Gerry Cheevers jokingly asked him after the game, "Will we be seeing you on the *Tonight Show* tonight?" Coach Don Cherry acknowledged that Wensink had come a long way in the previous two years. He said of John, "He was an absolutely brutal skater. Slow. Heavy. Couldn't turn. Just brutal. Two years ago he could not shoot the puck. He couldn't handle the puck."

Two years' worth of practice in the NHL certainly made a difference in the career of John Wensink.

* * *

One of the more notorious incidents involving Wensink occurred on December 1, 1977 in a game against the North Stars in Boston. In the third period of a game, the Bruins would win 4-2, John pummeled Alex Pirus, then began having a verbal exchange with players on the Minnesota bench. He skated over to within five feet of where the opponents were sitting and gestured to all of them to "come on." He waited a moment, and realizing there would be no takers, waved his hands in disgust and skated away.

Asked about the incident after the game he said, "They never said a word to me" when he invited them out to fight.

EDDIE WESTFALL

Boston sports fans are all too familiar with the way the story goes: the noteworthy and versatile athlete who has been part of the team's recent success is transferred to a New York team and the Boston team receives no players in return. The New York team goes on to great success in the next decade-plus, while the Boston team goes on a decades-long championship drought.

Right winger and occasional defenseman Ed Westfall was a member of the Bruins from 1961 to 1972. He had played an important role in the Stanley Cup championships of 1970 and 1972, but just days after winning the 1972 Cup, Westfall was allowed to be picked in the expansion draft by the New York Islanders. The Islanders went on to win four Stanley Cups in their first 12 years of existence, while the Bruins have not won since 1972.

Could the Bruins' subsequent championship drought be "the curse of Eddie Westfall?"

ROSS "LEFTY" WILSON

In yet another instance of the Bruins utilizing a spare goaltender, this time they had to reach behind the Red Wings' bench for a replacement. Detroit's assistant trainer, 38-year-old "Lefty" Wilson, who had been used twice on an emergency basis in the past few years by both the Red Wings and Canadiens, and would be wearing the Bruins sweater on December 29, 1957.

Eight minutes into the first period that night in Detroit, Bruins goalie Don Simmons separated his shoulder, and the pudgy Wilson was pressed into service. He performed admirably, allowing only one goal in the 1-1 tie, his final stint in an NHL contest.

HAL WINKLER

One of the very early goaltending standouts for the Bruins, Winkler played in net for the team from 1926 through 1928. During the 1927-28 season, his final in the NHL, he set a team record for shutouts of 15 that still stands.

When the Bruins won the Stanley Cup the season after Winkler's departure, he was honored by having his name engraved on the Cup along with the members of the 1928-1929 team, and was listed as "sub-goaltender."

BIBLIOGRAPHY

BOOKS

Booth, Clark. (1998). *Boston Bruins: Celebrating 75 Years.* Tehabi.

Bucyk, Johnny. (1972). *Hockey in my Blood.* Scribner's.

Cherry, Don & Fischler, Stan. (1982). *Grapes.* Spike.

Devaney, John. (1972). *We Love You Bruins.* Sport Magazine Press.

Diamond, Dan (Editor). (2000). *Total Hockey—Second Edition.* Total Sports Publishing.

Esposito, Phil, & Esposito, Tony. (1971). *The Brothers Esposito.* Hawthorn.

Fischler, Stan. (1969). *Bobby Orr and the Big, Bad Bruins.* Dell.

Fischler, Stan. (2001). *Boston Bruins: Greatest Moments and Players.* Champaign: Sports Publishing.

Green, Ted, & Hirschberg, Al. (1971). *High Stick.* Dodd, Mead & Co.

McFarlane, Brian. (1999). *Original Six: The Bruins.* Stoddart.

Park, Brad, & Fischler, Stan. (1971). *Play the Man.* Warner.

Sinden, Harry, & Grace, Dick. (1976). *The Picture History of the Boston Bruins.* Bobbs-Merrill.

Vautour, Kevin. (1997). *The Bruins Book.* ECW Press.

MAGAZINES

The Hockey News
The Sporting News
Hockey Digest
Sports Illustrated
Sport Magazine

NEWSPAPERS

Boston Globe
Boston Herald
Boston Post
Boston Record
New York Times

PHOTO CREDITS

Steve Babineau/Sports Action Archives pages 18, 22, 31, 38, 43, 45, 52, 56, 71, 83, 85, 129, 134, 139

Steve Babineau pages 61, 99, 107, 117, 152

Kevein Vautour collection page 9

Al Ruelle pages 27, 35, 40, 109, 111, 149

Boston Globe pages 12, 14, 146

AP Photo/Winslow Townson page 107